1,000

G

E

A PERIGEE BOOK
Published by the Penguin Group
Penguin Group (USA) Inc.
375 Hudson Street, New York, New York 10014, USA
Penguin Group (Canada), 90 Eglinton Avenue East, Suite 700, Toronto, Ontario M4P 2Y3, Canada
(a division of Pearson Penguin Canada Inc.)
Penguin Books Ltd., 80 Strand, London WC2R 0RL, England
Penguin Group Ireland, 25 St. Stephen's Green, Dublin 2, Ireland (a division of Penguin Books Ltd.)
Penguin Group (Australia), 250 Camberwell Road, Camberwell, Victoria 3124, Australia
(a division of Pearson Australia Group Pty. Ltd.)
Penguin Books India Pvt. Ltd., 11 Community Centre, Panchsheel Park, New Delhi—110 017, India
Penguin Group (NZ), Cnr. Airborne and Rosedale Roads, Albany, Auckland 1310, New Zealand
(a division of Pearson New Zealand Ltd.)
Penguin Books (South Africa) (Pty.) Ltd., 24 Sturdee Avenue, Rosebank, Johannesburg 2196, South Africa

Penguin Books Ltd., Registered Offices: 80 Strand, London WC2R 0RL, England

Cover art and design by Ben Gibson.
Text design by Tiffany Estreicher.

First edition: October 2006

Library of Congress Cataloging-in-Publication Data

Weidman, Sarah.
Gifted : 1,000 gift ideas for everyone in your life / Sarah Weidman.
p. cm.
ISBN 0-399-53299-4
1. Shopping. 2. Gifts. 3. Web sites—Directories. I. Title.
TX335.W355 2006
381'.45—dc22
2006049488

PRINTED IN THE UNITED STATES OF AMERICA

10 9 8 7 6 5 4 3 2 1

Most Perigee Books are available at special quantity discounts for bulk purchases for sales promotions, premiums, fund-raising, or educational use. Special books, or book excerpts, can also be created to fit specific needs. For details, write: Special Markets, The Berkley Publishing Group, 375 Hudson Street, New York, New York 10014.

To my parents, Judy and Russell,
for their years of unconditional love and support, creative inspiration, and generous gifts.

ACKNOWLEDGMENTS

I'd like to thank everyone who provided me with the advice, guidance, support, encouragement, and love I needed to write this book.

To my mom and dad, who eased my mind of many concerns and encouraged me while I checked out of my regular life to make this happen. To Baba Lil, for constantly boosting my ego. To my sister Jill, for her creativity, and my brother-in-law Gideon, for the support. To my aunt Linda, for her journalistic inspiration and helpful introductions. Thanks to Jennifer Litwin, author of *Furniture Hot Spots Coast to Coast* and *The Best Furniture Buying Tips Ever*, for her generosity with contacts and advice. Big props to Michael Seligman, owner of Bamboo Colony (the most fabulous furniture store in Los Angeles), for his editorial help and genius ideas. To my agent, Melissa Flashman, and my editor, Christel Winkler, for their enthusiasm for this book concept! Special shout-out to my amazing friends who have all contributed to the creation of this book in one way or another. And *so many thanks* to all of my friends and family—and Jill's many friends—who helped me by tossing their own great gift ideas into the *Gifted* pot of goodies.

experienced this same frustration. We inherently want to make people happy, and giving them something to treasure is a way to do just that. So I took it upon myself to ease the difficulties of gift giving for all of us. Use this book as a reference guide for your shopping convenience. You'll be introduced to products, services, and websites you may never have known existed, and hopefully, the suggestions will open up a whole new way of thinking when buying gifts.

Here's where to start: The next time you need to buy a gift, ask yourself some basic questions about the recipient: Are they adolescent or mature? Funky or conservative? A boss or your spouse? Once you narrow your giftee down to some general personality traits, dig deeper, because no individual can be categorized into a single persona. Does your gadget geek boss also love to travel? Does it look like your athletic sixteen-year-old niece will blossom into a gourmet chef? Is your know-it-all best friend obsessed with both Hollywood movies and his new dog? Break down their interests and choose one to focus on as the theme of your gift—you will not only get your "chore" done quickly, but you'll be surprised at how many fantastic gift options there are for everyone in your life. Then, finally, flip to the chapter in this book that best fits the profile of your recipient, ıake a decision, and you're done.

Here are some helpful hints to keep in mind as you read book:

'hen you go to a website to look at a recommended ', if you're not able to start shopping immediately off ıome page, look for a button that may say some- like Shop Online, Store, or Retail, and click on it ı shopping.

CONTENTS

INTRODUCTION

What makes the perfect present? Is there even such a thing as a "perfect" present? When it comes to buying gifts, we've all been stuck asking in frustration, "What the hell am I supposed to get!?!" Shopping for a gift shouldn't feel like a bullet point on your dreaded to-do list; it doesn't have to be a chore. Trust me—it's not difficult to find a gift that will stand out and make a lasting impression.

I wrote *Gifted: 1,000 Gift Ideas for Everyone in Your Life* because I got tired of picking up last-minute gifts th[illegible] were bland and impersonal. Several years ago, I obses[illegible] compulsively started keeping lists of different gi[illegible] I thought would be perfect for my friends, fami[illegible] leagues. I'd jot notes to myself, tear out pag[illegible] zines; I even tried to create an Excel sprea[illegible] findings straight. But, like most people[illegible] around the house, where they wo[illegible] disappear altogether. And then [illegible] I'd end up buying yet anoth[illegible] self for falling back on the [illegible]

As I set out to get organize[illegible]

- Once you're at the site's shopping page, look for a Search window and enter either a key word(s) from the product name or a description of the item. It should be able to locate what you're looking for. If there isn't a search engine available, start looking in the category that best fits that product.

- If you find the product and discover you don't like it, use the recommendation as inspiration, and tailor the idea to suit your recipient. You can search the Internet for similar products that may better suit what you're looking for, or hit some local retailers who may carry a comparable product.

- Prices listed in this book are for the products only and most of the time don't include shipping and handling costs. Order early, because the sooner you need the gift, the more expensive it will be for rushed shipping and handling. In addition, I've included a price key to help guide you to the right purchase. Please note the following ranges:

🎁	Up to $25
🎁🎁	From $26 to $75
🎁🎁🎁	From $76 to $150
🎁🎁🎁🎁	From $151 to $500
🎁🎁🎁🎁🎁	Over $500

- You should only make a purchase if you have confidence in the site and feel secure about the product you're choosing to buy. If you are at all suspicious, investigate. I've found that most websites have a customer service e-mail address or phone number, and their reps are usually very responsive when you ask a question. As much as I would love to have tried each and every one of these gift suggestions, I couldn't, so it's your responsibility to feel comfortable with the purchases that you make.

- The Internet is a fluctuating marketplace. If you discover a site or gift suggestion is no longer available, use a search engine to track down the item elsewhere—try putting in the brand name of the product or a description of what it is—and it's likely it will pop up on another site.

You'll be surprised at how many fabulous things are available on the Internet. And the best part is you won't have to fight crowds to shop! Every year, more and more people are taking advantage of the convenience of online shopping. I hope this book helps you discover the perfect gifts—or at least some inspiration—for the people in your life. Now start shopping!

THE SWEET SIXTEEN

The Sweet Sixteen is trapped at a crossroads where she's too old to pout for attention and too young to break free. Her parents want her to start thinking about college; she just hopes to get asked to the prom. So it's no surprise if a mild identity crisis occurs. The Sweet Sixteen may not have figured out where she's headed in life, but she *has* determined the more important issue: what is officially cool today. Here's a shopping cheat sheet: she wants the trendy cosmetics featured in this month's *In Style* or *Lucky* magazine. She adores anything with her name on it, from personalized tank tops to trinkets to totes. And she looooves her BFFs, so nothing beats a group experience that will create memories "2 share 4ever." The Sweet Sixteen feels confused, distressed, and even panicky at times—but when she opens a box to reveal the hottest bangle bracelet in town, she'll forget all about next week's SATs.

Swarovski "Bling" Monogrammed Compact

www.letscrystalit.com 🎁🎁🎁

Swarovski crystal oval shaped compact with two mirrors can be customized with any initial on the front.

Classic Tiffany's Heart Tag Key Ring

www.tiffany.com 🎁🎁/small

Made of sterling silver, this classic heart key ring tag can be engraved with initials—perfect for her own keys to the car!

Down-Filled Monogrammed Bed Rest Pillow

www.thecompanystore.com 🎁🎁🎁🎁/pillow + monogram

She can do homework in comfort with a soft, personalized pillow with back and arm support.

Unusual Yarns

www.kpixie.com 🎁+

For the budding knitters you know, get them a gift certificate to this site, which sells hard-to-find yarns.

Jelly Bath Tub Soak Gift Pack

www.jellybath.com 🎁🎁🎁/5-pack gift set

Jelly Bath is a tub soak that thickens into a jelly for a unique spa experience. The Variety Pack Five Tub Soaks gift set includes scents of lavender, strawberry, milk, mint, and lemongrass.

Meringues for the Memories

www.justmeringues.com 🎁🎁/100 cookies

These flavorful and colorful meringues are sweet treats that feature a personalized message sticking out of each one. Unique flavors include cinnamon, toffee crunch, and pumpkin spice.

Pajamagram

www.pajamagram.com 🎁🎁+

A pajama set that comes in an organza hatbox, lavender sachet, Do Not Disturb sign, personalized gift card, and decorative shipping box.

Custom-Designed Charm Bracelet

www.linksoflondon.com 🎁🎁🎁🎁+

Select from gold or silver, and choose which charms you want to attach to the bracelet from a complete charm catalog.

Sign Up with the Circus

www.damnhot.com/trapeze prices vary

Sign her up for trapeze classes; site provides a listing of trapeze classes in the United States.

Stitch-It Kit

www.sublimestitching.com 🎁

Something to get started with . . . Stitch-It Kit includes embroidery hoop, embroidery needle, seven-color floss palette, two tea towels, and thirty-five patterns.

The Everything Item

www.missakit.com 🎁

For the girl on the go. The pocket-sized Miss A Kit has a flashlight, keychain, needle and thread, perfume bottle, mirror, pillbox, knife, and more.

Customized License Plate

www.customlicenseplates.com 🎁

The plate symbolizes her new freedom on the road. Select a

state to represent and customize your own message up to ten characters (including spaces). Not authorized by the DMV.

Personalized Pencils

www.lillianvernon.com

Set of thirty #2 pencils with a name or saying on each. Can select from gold/silver, primary colors, pastels, black, or natural.

Personalized Cartoon

www.cowboychuck.com

/framed 8 × 10

Order a cute custom cartoon drawing of her with her name in a particular scene or favorite activity.

Poire Cell Phone Carrier

www.shopcitygirl.com

Poire carriers perfectly hold any cell phone and come in a variety of fabulous fabric styles.

Custom Photo Journal

www.cafepress.com

Make your own customized 160-page wire-bound journal that features a photo of her and her pals.

Portrait Studio

www.searsportrait.com

Treat her and her friends to a portrait session and photos at Sears. The gift recipient pays no session fees and can choose her favorite poses and sizes.

Croquet Set

www.brookstone.com

Be a Heather . . . this croquet set has an attractive, rosewood finish and includes six mallets, six polypropylene balls, nine steel wickets, two end posts, and a convenient wheel-around caddy.

One-of-a-Kind Lip Gloss

www.cosmeticmall.com

For customized lip color, Colorlab's Make Your Own Lip Gloss Kit comes with frosts, colors, and flavors to make up to six lip glosses.

Ice Cream Party!

www.benandjerrys.com

Send six pints of ice cream and a party pack to serve it with, because if you can't be at the party, then make the party. Select any six flavors for $54.95, then for an additional $11, include disposable Ben & Jerry's napkins, bowls, spoons, and Ben & Jerry's Perfect Ice Cream Scoop for serving.

Subscription to *Lucky* Magazine

/year

www.luckymag.com

This is the shopping guide to die for—the bible for all teen girls.

Sassy Telephone

www.fantasyphones.com

The TeleMania Hot Lips telephone is perfect for a gabfest.

Designer Makeup Brushes

www.eluxury.com

🎁🎁🎁

Trish McEvoy's Makeup-to-Go Set is stocked with five essential professional brushes, and comes in an adorable pink case.

"Jeweled" Swarovski Bling Pens

www.blueabaco.com

🎁🎁

The fabulous Swarovski Pen brings some sparkle to every writing moment. This "jewel"-encrusted ballpoint makes even the most mundane tasks fun.

Customized Crystallized Clothes

www.rhinestonerevival.com

🎁🎁

So easy—just pick your item of clothing (undies, sweats, tees), then pick your preferred font, then pick your Swarovski crystal color, and she's got a fancy-schmancy customized sparkly gift item.

Towel Checkers

www.beachstore.com

🎁🎁

This big terry beach blanket doubles as a checkerboard. Game pieces come in a separate bag.

Scented Pen

www.brightbluemoon.com

🎁

As you write, an Aroma Write Pen releases essential oils and gives off a fragrant scent. The pens come in six therapeutic scents: eucalyptus, lavender, ylang-ylang, chamomile, rosemary, and patchouli.

iPod Jacket

www.vickerey.com 🎁🎁🎁

This workout zip-up jacket conveniently comes with a built-in pocket on the upper sleeve for an iPod.

LoLLIA Concrete Perfume

www.beauty.com 🎁

Easy scent to toss in your purse for those on the go! LoLLIA concrete perfume comes in Sugar Blossom and is held in a decorated tin.

Hand-Beaded Slippers

www.twoladies.net 🎁🎁

Fluffy, hand-washable Fanciful Soles slippers are hand-beaded in colorful, fun, and whimsical themes.

Lip Plumpers

www.bellabeauty.net 🎁

Bella Beauty Lip Plumpers come in shimmery lights and sultry dark glosses, each in a set with three tubes. Glosses are infused with cinnamon and honey to plump the puckers.

Beach Mat Set

www.homebodyheaven.com 🎁

Bright plastic beach mat comes paired with a matching beach tote.

Mixo Cards

www.zolo.com 🎁

She'll get fifteen colorful cards and envelopes along with

forty-eight mixostickers to create a mix and match of her own personalized stationery.

Groove Master Stereo Messenger Bag

www.mosmyownspace.com 🎁🎁🎁

Plug in an iPod or CD player, and this messenger bag with two speakers turns into a boom box. Comes in white, black, pink, or green.

Fun Lap Desks

www.divadecor.com 🎁

These lap desks will add a splash of color to any homework assignment. The solid plastic top sits on top of a cushy pillow and has a built-in cup holder.

Kitson Coin Purse

www.shopkitson.com 🎁🎁

L.A.'s hot boutique Kitson presents coin purses! Made of leather, they are studded with rhinestones in the shape of a heart with wings. They are available in seafoam, pink, or purple; 6" × 4¼"; and have a zipper closure.

THE FIRST ANNIVERSARY DUET

Oh . . . the pressures of a first wedding anniversary. What to get? Where to go? How can this be turned into one hell of a special day for the love of your life? The first anniversary is a landmark achievement: you guys made it through the dreaded year one of marriage and have emerged shaken, if not stirred. Mark this moment and celebrate with something you two will never forget. Toss yourselves out of a hot air balloon while tied together with a bungee cord. Shoot a private home movie that has nothing to do with your weekend barbecue. Present your sweetheart with something personal, and follow this advice: if it can be given to someone else, throw it back and try again. You're setting a precedent here, and to be honest, there are expectations to be met. Channel your inner cupid and put the conventional couples to shame. If you play your cards right, this should be the last first anniversary of your life.

Panty-of-the-Month Club

www.panties.com +

This is definitely not something she'd buy for herself. Choose a three-, six-, or twelve-month subscription, and each month she'll receive a sexy panty and bra set. But wait, there's more! Each month, the gift-wrapped selection comes with bonus treats like perfume, chocolates, and sachets.

Chocolate Perfume

www.aftelier.com / ¼ oz. bottle

It's a chocolate lover's dream—to smell like it all day long. Aftelier Cacao is a hand-crafted chocolate perfume made from the best Scharffen Berger cocoa beans from Venezuela and Madagascar with exquisite Tahitian vanilla. Add in some jasmine, blood orange, and pink grapefruit, and you've got one sensual-smelling body.

Costumes

www.anytimecostumes.com +

Embrace your inner superhero and get a costume when it's not Halloween. Go for a sexy outfit—try a candy striper or bunny—or even the Maiden of Darkness. For the two of you, get the sexy Pharaoh ($49.99) and Cleopatra ($37.50).

Kama Sutra Music

www.tantra.com

Nothing beats sweet lovin' to the sounds of *Kama Sutra.* This sound track to the film *Kama Sutra: A Tale of Love* will set the mood for an intimate evening.

Smittens

www.smittens.biz

Now you can hold hands in the warmth of a shared mitten. You get two regular mittens and one Smitten.

A Year of Flowers

www.calyxandcorolla.com

Let her know every month that you're thinking of her. Select from a number of themes including tropicals, orchids, plants, or just regular flowers.

Fondue for Two

www.quelobjet.com

This romantic mini fondue kit comes with Belgian chocolate, a 3.5" fondue pot and stand, a candle, and two forks. Bring your own goodies to dip.

Bedroom Adventure Gear

www.theliberator.com

The Liberator is a wedge-shaped ramp designed to heighten sexual experiences. Barbra Streisand used one when teaching in *Meet the Fockers.*

Mile-High Kit

www.guyshop.com

For your next adventure as a couple, let loose high in the sky with a discreet mile-high kit. Kit contains condoms, lubricant, massage oil, a small metal vibrator, and some other titillating accessories.

Bikini Art Kit

www.justkittyng.com

Designing a private heart, arrow, star, tulip, and more for your sweetheart is one way to get close. Kit comes with stencils, a small comb, and scissors.

Dance Pole

www.lilmynx.com

The Original Lil' Minx portable stripping poles are easy to install anywhere, including in the center of your living room. Poles come in a range of colors.

Personalized Romance Novel

www.torridromance.com

Choose from among five private romantic novels that immortalize you and your lover forever in print. You provide the personalized details and get an authentic paperback novel that features you and your lover as the hero and heroine.

Double Sleeping Bag

www.sonomaoutfitters.com

Cozy up by a campfire with the Slumberjack Bonnie & Clyde sleeping bag built for two.

Learn Together

www.greatamericandays.com +

Select a location and sign up for private lessons for the two of you in anything from bull riding to rock climbing to surfing.

Ballroom Dancing

www.arthurmurray.com prices vary

Learn rumba, fox-trot, waltz, swing, salsa, cha-cha, and tango with your baby at an Arthur Murray dance studio. This site will help you find a studio in the United States. Cost varies by type of class and number of lessons.

Hire a Personal Chef

www.personalchefsearch.com prices vary

Select your meal, and a personal chef will show up with all the ingredients and hardware to cook up a very romantic, very private dining experience in your own home. This search engine will help you find independent chefs who offer these services in your area.

Hire a Skywriter

www.flysigns.com prices vary

Send a love note that everyone can read.

Do-It-Yourself Adult Movie Kit

www.epartyunlimited.com 🎁

Always thought about making your own steamy movie but never knew how to get started? The Do-It-Yourself Adult Movie Kit comes with script ideas, an erotic music CD, massage oil, pocket-sized body massager, and genuine movie clapper.

Make a Masterpiece

www.mydavinci.com 🎁🎁

Professional artists insert your faces into art masterpieces like Leonardo DaVinci's *Adam and Eve.*

Commemorative Wine Bottle

www.weddingwinesource.com

Create a special bottle of wine to commemorate this anniversary. You send in whatever image and text you want on the bottle's label; designers put it all together.

Build Your Own Photo Book

www.ofoto.com

At Ofoto, you send in your photos and captions, and they'll assemble a hardcover bound coffee table book. You can customize the layout and choose an exterior finish.

Roses with a Message

www.speakingroses.com

Declare your love by printing a special message on each individual rose.

Sexy and Slinky Alter Ego

www.trashy.com 

Trashy Lingerie in Los Angeles has a reputation for carrying a wide assortment of slinky and sexy costumes for her. They come with the full outfit, whether it includes a bra or corset or thong and tiny skirt. They also sell the essential hats and extras to make the getup perfectly assembled. There are endless themes to choose from: sexy pirate, bar wench, bondage kitty, Robin Hood, and many more.

Frederick's of Hollywood Marabou Slippers

www.fredericks.com

Sexy satin slip-on stilettos from the legendary Frederick's of Hollywood have three-inch heels and a hot feathery poof on top. Available in white, champagne, black, red, and pink.

"I ❤ U" Bud Vase Set

www.patinastores.com 🎁

This set of three perfect little bud vases have a white exterior and a red interior and on each say either "I" or "❤" or "U." Fill them with flowers to make this a special gift.

Oxford Backpack for Two

www.shiptheweb.com 🎁🎁

The Picnic at Ascot Oxford Backpack for Two comes with everything necessary to guarantee a romantic outdoor picnic. Insulated backpack keeps food cool, and durable canvas exterior with all sorts of pockets makes it easy to carry. Comes with a place setting for two, wood cutting board and cheese knife, salt and pepper shakers, corkscrew, cotton napkins and tablecloth, and a detachable wine carrier.

Personalized Wine Box

www.giftdistrict.com 🎁🎁

This customized wine box is made of solid wood and can be personalized on the lid with two lines of text—up to twenty-five characters on each line. Holds a standard bottle of wine—wine not included.

Candy Bra and G-String

www.gasworks.com 🎁/each

Some people like the candy necklaces; others . . . candy lingerie. Made like those innocent necklaces, the candy bra and candy G-string are tasty and tempting.

Christofle Champagne Straws

www.vivre.com 🎁🎁🎁

Très magnifique! Sip some bubbly through these 13" Christofle silver champagne straws and live it up in style. Set comes with two straws packaged in a pouch inside a green Christofle box.

Handsome Devil Mug

www.ournameismud.com 🎁

Red ceramic mug with horns has “Handsome Devil” hand painted on it.

Our First Bondage Kit

www.goodvibes.com 🎁🎁

It seems so innocent when presented in a cute little kit . . . but don’t let that throw you off. Our First Bondage Kit is meant to lure you into naughtiness. Kit comes with black fabric blindfold and fabric wrist and ankle cuffs with Velcro latches and nylon bondage extensions.

Intimo Men’s Silk Pajamas

www.saks.com 🎁🎁🎁🎁

He’ll feel sexy in these luxury striped silk pajamas in navy or black. Button-front top and drawstring bottoms.

THE PET LOVAH

Roll over, Fido, there's a new breed in town. Gone are the days where pets check into a kennel; now they have the option to lodge at luxury pet resorts that boast fabulous wading pools with waterfalls and outrageous suites with themes like the Magic Kingdom.

Somewhere along the way, "man's best friend" became "my little princess," and the amount of money spent on canine couture rivals the budget of a Third World nation. Today's pooches demand an exclusive lifestyle, so they're showered with rhinestone collars, designer coats, and chichi shoes. I mean really, why should precious paws pad the pavement when they can be outfitted in a pair of doggie UGGs? And then there are the first-class services available like emotional balancing massages, "peticures," even psychic readings. It's a bit much, but is that so wrong? After all, these pets provide their owners with unconditional love, constant companionship and support, and a reason to spend money on someone other than themselves. For that alone, they've earned every overpriced chew toy they've chomped.

CD for the Dogs

www.petcds.com 🎁

A music CD designed specifically for a dog's taste in music. *Songs to Make Dogs Happy!* was created with help from a real intuitive animal communicator.

Dog Flotation Vest

www.outdoorplay.com 🎁🎁

Never have to worry about your doggie drowning with a Ruff Wear K-9 Float Coat. You wear one. Why shouldn't they?

Pet Stroller

www.metropawlispetboutique.com 🎁🎁🎁🎁

The Fifth Avenue Pet Stroller SUV is the Rolls-Royce of pet strollers. It comes with chrome-plated wickets and stroller body, optional chrome license plate with your pet's name, a faux-fur pad, cup holder, removable carrier, rear safety brakes, and reflecting safety lights.

Orthopedic Pet Beds

www.pemadesign.com 🎁🎁

Pets get old, too, so this bed is designed to make their later years more comfortable. Filled with buckwheat hulls, the bed easily conforms to the contours of your pet's body to ensure a pain-free slumber. Bed comes in three sizes.

Monthly Dogliveries

www.threedog.com 🎁/month

Treat your doggie to a monthly gourmet treat. The Original Lucky Dog 12 Month Club will send your pup a different flavor of Bark 'n Fetch Cookies—a three-pound bag plus a surprise bakery treat of the month.

Customized Doghouses

www.lapetitemaison.com 🎁🎁🎁🎁🎁

Exclusive luxury doghouses that can be custom built to look like your own home.

Ionic Bath Massage Pet Brush

www.sharperimage.com 🎁🎁

This pet brush works to reduce pet dander, loosen tangles, and deodorize your cat or dog. Plus they're treated to a quickie massage.

Gucci Dog Bag

www.gucci.com 🎁🎁🎁🎁🎁

Dog carrier with signature web handles, double zip side opening, removable and washable interior cushion, and short leash with clip attached.

Gucci Dog Tag

www.gucci.com 🎁🎁🎁

Circular sterling silver *G* dog pendant with "Gucci dog" inscribed.

The Beetle Pet Sofa

www.divapaws.com 🎁🎁🎁

Let them mess up their own furniture . . . in fluffy style. Sofa comes in eight assorted colors.

Faux Fur Coat

www.superpetshop.com 🎁🎁🎁🎁

Faux fur coat for the dog—the ultimate luxury coat for the fashionista pooch.

LV Dog Collar

www.eluxury.com 🎁🎁🎁🎁

Louis Vuitton's monogrammed dog collar keeps style on a leash.

Bronzed Paw Print

www.pawsofendearment.com 🎁🎁

Customized pet paw plaque with a side-by-side photo of the dog and bronzed paw print.

The Pet Umbrella

www.coolstuffcheap.com 🎁

Keeps your pet dry and comfortable in wet weather. An umbrella leash with hook attaches easily and quickly to your pet's collar or harness.

New Puppy Starter Kit

www.handsnpaws.com 🎁🎁

Comes with poop bags, toys, treats, spa samples, and more.

Outward Hound Pet Carrier

www.doggy-gifts.com 🎁+

Keep your pet secure and content against your body with the Outward Hound carrier. It's the BABYBJÖRN of the puppy world.

Burberry Dog Coat

www.henryandlulu.com 🎁🎁🎁🎁

That lovely plaid belongs on everyone.

Doggie All-Terrain Boots

www.ruffwear.com 🎁🎁

Stylishly protect paws from all surfaces—rough, hot, slick, frozen—with 3D Bark 'n Boots.

Tee Pee Hound Lounge

www.henryandlulu.com 🎁🎁🎁🎁

The Tee Pee Hound Lounge will become your dog's new favorite hangout. Comes in khaki green with orange trim and has a fleece pad inside.

Designer Chew Toys

www.muttropolis.com 🎁/each

You'll enjoy them, too . . . Chewy Vuitton shaped like a Louis Vuitton, Jimmy Chew shaped like a sexy heel, Chewnel #5 perfume, and Sniffany & Co. in that fabulous blue box tied with a white ribbon, plus more styles and sets available.

Dog Cologne

www.pawson5th.com 🎁

Because dogs should smell as good as they possibly can. Choose from Aramutts, CK-9, Pucci, and Miss Claybone.

Doggie UGG-like Booties

www.luluandluigi.com 🎁🎁🎁

Stylish and warm, these Fur Lilyboots suede booties with faux-fur lining have all the markings of a pampered pooch.

Personalized Adjustable Dog Collar

www.orvis.com 🎁

For those anti-rhinestone pups who still want their name on a collar, this simple and sturdy nylon collar with easy snap-on/off side-release buckle will do the job. You can personalize your pet's name and telephone number with up to seventeen characters including spaces on S/M; up to twenty-one characters including spaces on L/XL. Choose from nine different collar colors.

Painted Pet Portrait

www.jeffpetportraits.com 🎁🎁🎁+

Los Angeles–based artist Jeff Parise has found a market with his oil-on-canvas pet portraits. Jeff works from photographs and can usually turn a painting around in a week. Gift certificates are available. Framing is an additional $100.

Moc Croc Pet Bowls

www.tossdesigns.com 🎁🎁

This double pet bowl holder is made of easy-to-clean vinyl that looks just like croc and comes in pink, green, orange, or black. The cradled ceramic bowls stand 4" from the ground.

Subscription to *Hollywood Dog* Magazine

www.thehollywooddog.com 🎁/year

Hollywood Dog is published bimonthly and features pieces on doggie style, doggie wellness, and doggie obituaries. Articles will also dig deep and ask those important questions like "Dogs and cosmetic surgery . . . have we gone too far?"

Treat Jar

www.thefashionablepet.com

Cute Good Dog Bones ceramic treat jar keeps doggie treats fresh. Also available in a Good Kitty Treat Jar.

Furcedes Car Dog Bed

www.thedoggylama.com

It looks just like a hot convertible Mercedes, but your dog is at the wheel. Soft, comfy, and luxe, just like the real thing.

Spa Bathrobe for Dogs

www.ledoggiecouture.com

The Doggie Spa Robe is perfect for after the bath. It's made of a fabric that soaks up seven times its weight in water, so helps you keep your home dry. Comes in pink, blue, peach, and yellow.

Designer Dog Collar

www.upcountryinc.com

Choose from dozens of fashionable fabric colors in an array of patterns and styles.

Floral Dog Bowl

www.upcountryinc.com

The Flower Power ceramic dog bowl shows you care about your dog's dining dishes.

Boca Ultrasuede Wonderdog Bed

www.ledoggiecouture.com

The Boca Wonderdog bed is perfect for the modernist dog. Made with an Ultrasuede cover over a polyester foam pillow, the bed is extremely comfortable and resistant to crocking, pilling, fraying, stretching, and shrinking. Fabric can be cleaned with a damp cloth or at a dry cleaner. Cover comes in geranium, blueberry, midnight, and mango.

Slipper Bed

www.thedoggylama.com 🎁🎁🎁

Any dog will have a peaceful night's sleep in this pet bed shaped like a luxurious slipper with a faux-fur exterior. Inside is fleece-lined and removable and washable; comes in white fur or pink fur. Bonus: comes with its own newspaper-like chew toy.

Dog Friendly's Dog Travel Guide

www.dogfriendly.com 🎁

DogFriendly.com's United States and Canada Dog Travel Guides help find everything that's dog-friendly across the United States and Canada from accommodations to attractions to dog parks and beaches to highway guides.

Doggie Costumes

www.spoiledrottendoggies.com 🎁+

Just for the hell of it, how about bringing the dog along for Halloween? Doggie costumes range from tuxedos and bridal gowns to Darth Vader and Wonder Woman to Mickey Mouse and Snow White.

Doggie Necklace

www.charmingpetcharms.com 🎁🎁

The Le Fancy Bone Pearl Necklace is a strand of faux pearls with a rhinestone bone charm. Made for only the most upscale dogs.

Pink and Posh Dog Stole

www.thedoggylama.com

🎁🎁

This faux-fur pink pouf collar has a rhinestone heart charm dangle and is lined in pink satin.

And while the pet shopping biz is clearly for the dogs, there are also a few ways to spoil your feline friends.

Hidden Kitty Litter Box

www.hidnlitter.com

🎁🎁🎁

It looks like a plant in a terra-cotta holder, but only those in the know are aware that it's your cat's home away from home.

Cat Chew Toy

www.georgesf.com

🎁

Catnip toys in the shape of Chihuahuas and other small doggies.

Cat Calming Mat

www.thecatconnection.com

🎁

It's almost as nice as lying in the sun. Just microwave this mat, and your cat instantly has a warm spot to relax.

Cat Window Perch

www.thecatconnection.com

🎁🎁

For curious cats, the Cat Napper allows your kitties to chill in a hammock while peeking out the window to see what's going on outside. Adjustable to fit most sills and holds cats up to thirty-five pounds.

Potty Training Kitty

www.thecatconnection.com

If you didn't think it was possible, give it a shot—toilet train your cat. Replace your existing toilet seat with the CatSeat, which has shelves that hide the water below. When pushed, a paw-shaped button makes the shelves disappear and transforms the CatSeat back into a normal toilet seat for human use. Good luck.

Kitty Gym

www.catsplay.com

+

There are plenty of models to choose from—some have houses, perches, tubes, and more to play on with these Kitty Gyms. Think about all of the excitement and exercise your cat will have as a member of this exclusive club.

Kitty Treehouse

www.petedge.com

The Meow Town Kitty Treehouse Hideaway brings the outdoors in! Includes two tree climbing posts, a private treehouse, and a hammock for all those catnaps.

Slumber Pet Cabana

www.petedge.com

Or maybe a beach locale is more your style?

THE SPORTY ADVENTURER

The Sporty Adventurer is always ready for a challenge—if there's a mountain to mount, a river to raft, or a game to gear up for, these sporty types will likely be the first in line. While you're sleeping soundly in your cozy bed, they're already taking deep dewy morning breaths and heading off for the game. Basically, you lounge; they lunge. But that doesn't mean you can't support their active lifestyle. Send them on a glorious quest that offers up fresh tests for them to tackle. Track down the latest essentials and equipment that would make their next expedition more interesting. Or just give them an opportunity to take a break from the action by watching *other* people push themselves too hard. Sure, it's a little difficult keeping up with the Sporty Adventurer, but instead of resenting them for making you feel lazy, say "Thank you," because without them, you'd still think the world was flat and you wouldn't have an excuse to pig out on Super Bowl Sunday.

Digital Car Compass

www.travelproducts.com

🎁🎁

No more floating ball compasses on the dashboard—upgrade to a digital compass for an accurate and modern directional reading. The Wayfinder V100 electronically compensates for the magnetic fields generated by your vehicle and is battery-operated.

Sports Chair

www.presentdaygifts.com

🎁🎁

Lightweight, easy-to-carry portable chair is made of aluminum and heavy polyester and is padded in all the right places. Side pocket doubles as an organizer and other-side table is perfect for a drink.

Engraved Baseball Bat

www.abernook.com

🎁🎁

Personalized Rawlings Big Stick baseball bat is 34" in length and can be personalized with up to three lines of twenty characters per line.

Team Tie

www.tieguys.com

🎁+

For the avid sports fans, get them a tie that shows off their team spirit. Every team represented from the NFL, NBA, MLB, and NHL.

Remote Control Lantern

www.dickssportinggoods.com

🎁

Wenzel lantern operates off a fluorescent bulb and is remote controllable from up to twenty-five feet away. Bonus: It's waterproof and floats.

CamelBak Classic Water Pack

🎁🎁

www.rei.com

Stay hydrated with a water-filled backpack. Holds seventy ounces of liquid and makes it easy to sip with an over-the-shoulder straw.

Sports Cooler

🎁🎁

www.fansedge.com

Perfect for game days—a twelve-pack cooler with either your school's team logo or that of your favorite pro team.

Piece of a NASCAR car

🎁🎁+

www.fansedge.com

It's almost like being there—a photograph of a favorite NASCAR car is framed along with an actual metal piece of the race-used car and a name plaque of the driver.

Outdoor Stadium Seat

🎁

www.thesportsauthority.com

Forget hard bleachers; treat your bum to an outdoor bleacher seat with back. The GCI Outdoors Bleacher-Back Stadium Seat is easy to carry, and provides a soft cushion to sit on and firm support for your back.

Wristband Digital Clock

🎁

www.jockclock.com

Hate wearing a watch to the gym? JockClock is a sweat-band with a built-in digital watch so you can see how long you've been sweating.

SteriPEN Water Purifying Pen

www.magellans.com

🎁🎁🎁

Purify questionable water with a SteriPEN that gives off UV light for sterilization.

Restop Portable Toilets

www.magellans.com

🎁

Pop a squat responsibly. Restop 1 and 2 are easy-to-use bags made of a biodegradable blend of polymers that breaks down waste and turns it into a gel. Includes instructions, tissues, and antiseptic wipes.

Sting Extractor Kit

www.domsoutdoors.com

🎁

Good to have this around—Sawyer Extractor Kit is a recognized way to treat snakebites and bee stings.

Personal Headlamp

www.domsoutdoors.com

🎁

Priceton Tec Quest Headlamp is a hands-free alternative to a flashlight.

Triathlete's Best Friend

www.polarusa.com

🎁🎁🎁🎁

The Polar S625X watch determines heart rate and running and cycling data for a triathlon.

Runner's Relief

www.zipsnaturalsport.com

🎁🎁

Zip's All-Inclusive Gift Pack includes Sport Soap, Scab Dab, Sole Spray, Nip Stick, Sole Soak, and Muscle Rub.

All-in-One Sports Training Machine

www.onlinesports.com 🎁🎁🎁🎁🎁

The Bigfoot Machine is able to pitch any size ball, from baseball to football to soccer-ball size. It can throw a football one hundred yards in the air, it can toss a volleyball over the net in a soft toss fashion, it can put a variety of different spins to simulate real soccer conditions, and it can pitch a sinker, curve, slider, and fastball with ease.

Tilley Hat

www.tilley.com 🎁🎁

Practical hat for an outdoors person—the Tilley Lightweight LTM5 Hat provides good shading, is waterproof, and it's insured for life!

Race Car Driving Experience

www.1800bepetty.com 🎁🎁🎁🎁🎁 (Daytona)

NASCAR star Richard Petty has his own chain of driving schools around the nation. One package offered is the Daytona Experience. On the actual Daytona track, you get three sessions of training, instruction, and feedback from a real Pit Road Instructor and three opportunities to race laps.

Log Cabin Kit

www.conestogalogcabins.com 🎁🎁🎁🎁🎁

Build your own log cabin with a prefab kit. The Conestoga Kamping Cottage is a 12' × 12' room that comes complete with all the parts needed to build your own log cabin.

Sports Event

www.MLB.com prices vary

Give a friend two tickets to an upcoming sporting event.

Some major teams even offer undated gift certificates redeemable for any home game. For baseball fans, go to the Major League website and see what deals your favorite team offers—i.e., Mets Money is good at all food and beverage counters, restaurant areas, party facilities, souvenir stands, and ticket outlets at Shea Stadium.

Sports Memorabilia

www.onlinesports.com

Give a piece of sports history with jerseys, equipment, and gear autographed by favorite players from all sports. Each item of sports memorabilia comes with a certificate of authenticity.

Backpack Snacks

www.backpackerspantry.com

A grocery store for backpackers that offers meals packaged in little pouches ranging from No-Cook Beef Stroganoff with chicken noodle soup and pudding for dessert to scrambled eggs with bacon, potatoes, and orange drink.

Build-Your-Own Boot

www.timberland.com

At the Bootstudio, you start with the classic yellow Timberland boot and customize every detail to your own color and style preferences.

Football Slippers

www.onlyslippers.com

They can slip into the comfort of game day with the NixesSlippers football-shaped Touch Down slippers.

Mountain Hardwear Space Station

www.mgear.com 🎁🎁🎁🎁🎁

It's the ultimate party tent! Sleeping fifteen people comfortably, the nylon and aluminum-poled house features 304 feet of floor space, a nearly ten-foot ceiling, three doors, and five windows. The whole thing weighs fifty pounds packed into its duffel bag.

Instant Sports Hero

www.justmesports.com 🎁

This CD re-creates a sporting event with a professional announcer celebrating your friend as having won the game. Select from an actual U.S. pro team and you'll hear play-by-play game commentary, where your friend's name is mentioned around thirty times. Choose from basketball, baseball, football, soccer, hockey, and NASCAR.

Classic Camping Tool

www.shiptheweb.com 🎁

Stainless steel Kikkerland camping gadget has a fork, knife, bottle opener, and corkscrew in a compact size.

Laser Baseball

www.sharperimage.com 🎁🎁

Ever wonder how fast you can throw a baseball? This ball has a built-in system to measure the speed of a pitch in mph and displays the result in a convenient digital window.

LifeAid Sport

www.zelco.com 🎁

This palm-sized gadget will come in handy outdoors. It houses a shrill whistle for protection and calling, a compass, thermometer, and a dual-beam LED light with a strobe option for signaling.

National Geographic Travel Vest

www.nationalgeographic.com

This tan nylon field vest has nineteen pockets to store all travel needs: tickets, maps, passport, water bottle, and more. It is water-, stain-, and wrinkle-resistant.

ESPN All Sports Trivia Challenge

www.espnshop.com

ESPN board game features 1,500 questions in ten categories and pits sports fans against each other in a battle to be crowned champion.

Car Magnets

www.fridgedoor.com

Really want to show team spirit? Get one of these large team logo magnets designed to stick to the side of your car. Each item is approximately 12" and made of heavy-gauge magnetic vinyl.

Personalized Golf Caddy

www.giftdistrict.com

Sleek tan leather golf caddy has room for tees, a divot tool, and a ball marker with a single initial. Also comes with a four-ounce stainless steel flask, room for a cell phone, and a loop to attach to your bag. Item can be personalized.

Incredible Adventure

www.incredible-adventures.com prices vary

Kick it into high gear with an adrenaline-pumping, high-intensity adventure. Incredible Adventures offers opportunities for everything from Covert Ops Training to Offshore Rockets and Speedboat Racing to Battle Tank Games in a WW II Military Tank. Locations and prices vary depending on the adventure.

THE HAPPY HOMEMAKER

Once upon a time in high school, there was a required class called home economics. In that hour, a young lady learned what skills were necessary to be a good wife and run a swell home. Then one day, she decided to burn her bra and tossed home ec into the flames. The end.

Today, the course may be extinct, but the practices it preached have lived on. The Happy Homemaker has emerged gleefully empowered and gets great satisfaction from TV shows that dare to ask, "How Clean Is Your House?" then publicly humiliate those with dusty duvets. For them, daytime soaps are verbena and lavender. The Happy Homemaker craves accents that will make her house a home: stylish dinner party accessories, do-it-yourself projects to brighten up a room, one-of-a-kind edible treats to share with guests . . . essentially, anything that will help her maintain a well-oiled and fashionable abode. Our mothers and grandmothers may have been expected to maintain this lifestyle, but today's Happy Homemaker sees it as a challenge, not a chore.

Designer Garden Gnome

www.gadgeteerusa.com 🎁🎁🎁🎁

Yeah! Gnomes! If you're lonely, these guys will keep good company. Created by Philippe Starck for Kartell, the gnomes can hang out in the garden or be used as a seat or table.

Monogrammed Cocktail Napkins

www.ink-well.net 🎁/set of four

Classic and classy: 100 percent cotton cocktail napkins sporting a single initial.

Everyday BBQ Pit

www.napastyle.com 🎁🎁🎁🎁

Gigantic barbecue pit was invented for whipping up lots of food for enormous parties. It roasts up to four chickens, three pork rib slabs, two pork shoulders, or eighteen pounds of turkey. Just lay the meat on the grill, and the roaster slow-cooks dinner to perfection.

Best Furniture Buying Tips Ever!

www.amazon.com 🎁

Jennifer Litwin is a top consumer advocate in the home furnishings industry and has put together this useful book detailing what everyone should know when buying furniture.

Stainless Steel Master Grill Set

www.kitchenwaresetc.com 🎁🎁

Twenty-piece stainless steel set has all the forks, skewers, brushes, knives, tongs, and holders every great griller needs. Comes in a sexy aluminum carrying case.

Gourmet Tea-Scented Candles

www.sloanhall.com 🎁🎁

An entire room can smell like Darjeeling, red tea, or green tea with these posh and gorgeous Mariage Frères candles.

Mini Moc Croc Shaker

www.flipflopstyle.com 🎁

Eight-ounce party mini-shaker comes in orange, lime, blue, pink, or black and serves up cocktails in funky style.

Automatic Ice Cream Maker

www.deni.com 🎁🎁

Make your favorite ice creams in ten to twenty minutes. No salt needed; the specially designed canister does all the work. Just remove it from the freezer, pour in the ingredients, and you're ready to go.

Gucci Ice Cube Trays

www.gucci.com 🎁🎁🎁

Set of two trays comes in black rubber. The *G*-shaped pieces give new meaning to *ice*.

Deluxe Glass Etching Kit

www.misterart.com 🎁

Snazz up ordinary glass items with the Armour Deluxe Glass Etching Kit. The set comes with all necessary supplies including precut stencils, etching cream, cutting knife, and brush.

French Market Garden Kit

www.earthlygoods.com

Kit comes with ten different seeds—everything needed to grow a French Market Garden including mesculun salad mix, summer squash, baby carrots, and sweet cucumbers.

Pink Ladiez Tool Kit

www.fredflare.com

Hey ladiez, it's never too late to start building your dreams. For the handy gal, this tool kit contains hot pink screwdrivers, hammer, pliers, scissors, and more.

The Original Pink Tool Belt

www.pinktoolbelts.com

This heavy-duty suede tool belt helps her get the job done with her new tools in a sassy and feminine way. Four main nail/tool pockets and six smaller pockets fit every tool and necessity for home maintenance.

Tile Coaster Making Kit

www.dickblick.com

With the Tilano Fresco Coaster Making Kit, they can create their own tile coasters with some of their favorite photos. Makes four coasters that measure 4" × 4" × ⅜". Image transfer kit sold separately.

Fancy Dish Soap

www.thymes.com

Mandarin Coriander, Lavender Bergamot, Apricot Quince, and Kumquat Lime scented dish washing soap spice up ordinary dish washing.

Cocktail Candy

www.cocktailcandy.com 🎁/tin

Rim the glass of your favorite cocktail or smoothie with your favorite sugar flavor. The sugars are packaged in stylish round metal tins that can be used as a serving tray to rim the cocktail glass. Over twenty flavors including cranberry, coffee, grape, and apple.

Dinner Party Kit

www.traylorpapers.com 🎁🎁

Give them everything they need to throw a coordinated dinner party for ten. The Toccare Design Dinner Party Kit comes with invitations, note cards, menu cards, place cards, napkin rings, and vellum wrap.

Pretty Address Labels

www.iomoi.com 🎁🎁/120 labels

Personalized address labels with over fifty designs to choose from, including red coral, preppy stripe, argyle, robin's egg blue, cupcake, and dog.

Garden Clogs

www.plowhearth.com 🎁

Available in red, yellow, or blue, these garden clogs are made of waterproof rubber so they're super easy to clean.

Take-Out Menu Organizer

www.knockknock.biz 🎁🎁

The compulsively organized homeowner can keep menus filed and categorized for easy ordering. Kit includes binder, accessories pouch, six section dividers, thirty clear sleeves, an order-taking pad, a pad of ratings stickies, dry-erase pens for writing on clear sleeves, six interior pages with frequently called numbers, and an essay on the "Definitive History of Take-Out."

Glam Aprons

www.kitschnglam.com 🎁🎁

Vintage-styled aprons for the ultraswanky chef.

Make-Your-Own-Opoly Game

www.areyougame.com 🎁

They can control their own world by creating a game board with their personalized neighborhood. Game kit contains a game board, cards, money, dice, pawns, computer paper sets, paper and label set, publishing booklet, clip art guide, CD-ROM, and simple instructions.

Classic Soda Pop Stock

www.sodapopstop.com 🎁/each

Galco's Old World Grocery features a huge selection of gourmet and old-fashioned sodas like Moxie Cherry Cola, Faygo Original Rock & Rye, Jones Soda Company Vanilla Cola, Apple-Beer, and Borgnine's Coffee Soda.

A Cooking Class

www.surlatable.com 🎁🎁+

How much fun would it be to learn to cook your own gourmet meal? Sounds like a party waiting to happen.

Beautiful Cakes

www.lilyfieldcakes.com 🎁🎁🎁🎁

It's may be the prettiest cake package you'll ever send. Each cake from the Classic Collection comes in a luxurious upholstered container bedecked with fresh flowers and a charm.

Personalized Stamps

www.photostamps.com 🎁/sheet of 39¢ stamps

So they can mail bills with their faces smiling back off the stamp. Send in any photo, and it's turned into legal U.S. postage stamps. Single sheets contain twenty stamps.

Fondue Kit

www.williams-sonoma.com 🎁🎁🎁

You're not only giving a gift that will last, but you're providing a party theme. The All-Clad stainless steel pot comes with six stainless steel forks.

Faaaabulous Dish Gloves

www.discountcooking.com 🎁

Glovables' stylish dish gloves come in black rubber with leopard print, lace, or polka-dot cuffs or pink rubber with pink polka-dot cuffs. Do the dishes in style!

Martha Stewart's Hors d'Oeuvres Handbook

www.amazon.com 🎁🎁

It's the quintessential guide for every entertainer. This cookbook and handbook covers everything a homemaker needs to know about appetizers and hors d'oeuvres. Practical knowledge and recipes fill this 496-page bible.

Reusable Place Settings

www.crateandbarrel.com 🎁

The Grace Placetiles lend some formality to a dining table, but the handwritten names warm it up again. Set of six ceramic placetiles have a bead-patterned border and come with a dry-erase marker to write in your guests' names. Just wipe with a damp cloth to clean.

Cheese and Wine Lovers' Gift Set

www.kitchenetc.com 🎁🎁🎁🎁

This gorgeous gift set by Wüsthof includes three cheese knives with stainless steel blades for soft, hard, and Parmesan cheeses. It also comes with a waiter's corkscrew. All of the pieces are housed in an elegant bamboo case.

Elegant Sachet Trio

www.martinbarnettretail.com 🎁🎁

The Floral Sachet Trio is a threesome of mini silk sachets, all topped off with a delicate flower and filled with Martin Barnett's signature scent—Sage Flower—a blend of sandalwood, cedar wood, French sage, and myrrh. The trio comes in a lovely gift box (2" × 2" × 5") and a choice of three color combinations.

Gardener Intensive Hand Repair Kit

www.thymes.com 🎁🎁

By Thymes, this set of Gardener Hand Scrub and Hand Cream expertly cleans, moisturizes, and repairs.

Wall Decals

www.whatisblik.com 🎁🎁+

Dress a blank wall up with some prepared artwork that's

easy to apply (and remove)—just peel and stick. Multiple patterns and images available in different colors.

Bread Mixes

www.pelicanbayltd.com 🎁/mix

Make-your-own-bread mixes come packaged in corrugated tote bags with vintage artwork and are tied with a ribbon and mini grater. Flavors are: banana, zucchini, apple, and monkey breads.

Fancy Ice Cream Pint Holders

www.vivre.com 🎁🎁

No one should feel guilty for eating directly out of the pint; embrace the binge and eat from it in style. Drop any ice cream pint directly into one of these lovely containers and feel like you're being as proper as you need to be. Choose from mango wood or silver-plated.

Decorative Wall Bands

www.shoptwenty2.com 🎁🎁/package

It's an easy way to spice up a room. These patterned wall bands are prepasted strips of wallpaper that activate with water. The surface is washable—just wipe down to clean. Each package comes with a band that's fifteen feet long and thirteen inches wide. Choose from five different patterns, each in a variety of colors.

Gardener's Hip Watch

www.whiteflowerfarm.com 🎁🎁

This convenient gardener's watch is a water-resistant quartz timepiece that's less than two inches in diameter. The watch has numerals and military time symbols, an

Indiglo night-light dial, and is kept protected in a brown leather case that hooks onto your belt.

Letter Seal and Sealing Wax Set

www.letterseals.com 🎁+

A gift set of a special letter seal and sealing wax will come in handy when a letter is actually handwritten and not sent via e-mail. Choose a seal from a large selection and then select a color of wax.

Baguette Slicer

www.napastyle.com 🎁🎁

This wood tray has convenient slots that make it easy to slice a long baguette. Measures 29.5" × 5".

Stainless Steel Cookbook Stand

www.onlineorganizing.com 🎁🎁

This 12.5" × 10.5" × 2" sleek stainless steel cookbook stand has an adjustable back to support any size cookbook, an acrylic splash guard, and nonskid feet. Stand collapses for easy storage.

Chef Towels

www.kookootowels.com 🎁

Funny 100 percent cotton terry kitchen towels embroidered with a cute picture and the titles "Gourmet Chef" or "Crappy Cook."

Grab-and-Go Gift Sets

www.stonewallkitchen.com 🎁

These are easy tokens to give someone. The Grab-and-Go gift sets include a Vanilla Bundt Cake Mix with a jar of

White Chocolate Orange Sauce, or a Farmhouse Pancake and Waffle Mix with Amber Maine Maple Syrup. Five sets to choose from; all of them come wrapped in a clear bag with the appropriate kitchen utensil tied into the bow.

Customized Soaps

www.samsoap.com +

SÄM SOAP has a custom soap-making menu. Just select options from an extensive list: soap size and type, essential oils or fragrance, exfoliant ingredient, and moisturizer. And you can have the recipient's name or a message custom printed on the item. Gift certificates are also available if you want to leave the cooking to them.

Fabric Print Oval Tray

www.decorativethings.com

This tray comes in twelve gorgeous laminated fabric patterns. Measures approximately 9" × 13" and is dishwasher safe.

Magazine Cataloger

www.scanalog.com

If you are constantly collecting pages torn out of magazines, now there's a way to organize those thoughts. A computer program called Scanalog will store, catalog, and retrieve your favorite articles from your favorite magazines into a number of convenient categories.

Heirloom Garden Candle

www.paddywax.com 🎁🎁

Paddywax Candles have a perfect line of scents for the garden lover. Packaged in a gorgeous illustrated box, these one hundred–hour candles come in Brandywine Tomato, Cupani Sweet Pea, Florence Fennel, Moon & Stars Watermelon, and Squash Blossom.

THE GADGET GEEK

The Gadget Geek is an interesting paradox—gadgets are cool; geeks are not—but together, they make a very special person. They're the ones who valiantly come to your rescue when your computer crashes. They actually *own* one of those massage chairs you "try out" whenever you pass a Sharper Image. And they provide one-of-a-kind viewing experiences with their sixty-one-inch flat-screen plasma and Dolby 5.1 surround sound. Understandably, it's a challenge finding something original for the Gadget Geek, but you just have to get creative. Unusual spy equipment may not be something they'd get for themselves, but they'd get a kick out of getting it from you. Anything electronic that enhances their *other* electronics will definitely be treasured. And then there are the ambitious kits to immerse themselves in and go days without sleeping. Basically, if it involves assembly, a power source, or technical wizardry, you can be certain your Gadget Geek will love it . . . until it's time to upgrade. And then you know what to give them next year.

Solar-Powered Glow Globes

www.grandinroad.com 🎁🎁

Totally futuristic, these solar-powered MagicGlobe light spheres give a backyard or pool a supercool attitude. Not only do they stay lit in the dark for twenty-four hours, but these 5½" spheres are fine to lounge on a table or float on water.

Automatic Beverage Cooler

www.bestbuy.com 🎁🎁🎁

Cooper Cooler Rapid Beverage Chiller turns a can of cola from room temperature to cold in sixty seconds. Also warms quickly—good for baby bottles.

USB Mini Lava Lamp

www.thinkgeek.com 🎁

This tiny working lava lamp (5.8" × 1.7") plugs into a computer's USB port to power up the chill.

Spy Camcorder

www.sharperimage.com 🎁🎁🎁🎁

This secret camcorder is motion-controlled and hidden in a functional LCD clock. No one will ever know . . .

Home Professional Wireless Weather Station

www.weather.com 🎁🎁🎁

This supersleek Wireless Weather Station 9035 tells you the time and date, indoor and outdoor temperature/humidity, current moon phase, wind speed, and more.

Meade Telescopes

www.ritzcamera.com 🎁🎁🎁+

Explore the world . . . or your neighbors.

Cell Phone Sync

www.futuredial.com 🎁🎁

Edit and transfer data between your cell phone and Outlook or Outlook Express with FutureDial's SnapSync cell phone sync software. The single SnapSync Software CD is fully compatible with over 270 popular cell phones manufactured by most leading cell phone makers.

Secret Rock Music

www.livingthespalife.com 🎁🎁🎁🎁

If you want music outside but don't want to see the speakers, there's a speaker designed to look like a rock. The Rock Speaker is made from fiberglass-reinforced concrete, it's hand painted to look real, and is weatherproof and UV resistant.

Navigation System

www.tomtom.com 🎁🎁🎁🎁

Turn a handheld PDA into an in-car navigation system with the TomTom NAVIGATOR 5. Different programs exist for different handhelds. Comes with software to make the upgrades.

Night Vision Device

www.mossonline.com 🎁🎁🎁🎁

The Chameleon Night Vision Device takes any available light and amplifies it so you can see in the dark through the scope.

Sushi USB Memory Stick

www.dynamism.com 🎁🎁🎁/piece

This USB memory drive looks just like a piece of sushi and comes in several flavors. Available in 32MB or 128MB size.

Computer Cooler

www.targus.com 🎁🎁

The Targus Notebook ChillHub protects laptop computers from overheating and damaging your furniture by pulling heat away from the computer and padding the space underneath.

Portable Satellite Radio

http://shop.sirius.com 🎁🎁🎁

Sirius Satellite Radio's Starmate Replay Radio offers a unique compact design that integrates into a car's interior. The replay can store up to forty-four hours of content.

Digital Photo Receiver

www.discoverystore.com 🎁🎁🎁 + $10/month subscription fee

For a low monthly subscription fee, the Digital Photo Receiver will receive and display up to thirty new pictures a day. No computer is needed—just plug in the power cord and the phone line. The receiver is designed to look like a 5 × 7 picture frame.

Colorcalm DVD

www.colorcalm.com 🎁

It's a DVD that's looped to play a continuously changing colored sky with clouds. Meant to create an atmosphere, it can turn any TV or computer monitor into a calming display.

Global Travel Radio

www.tivoliaudio.com

The SongBook AM/FM Alarm Clock Travel Radio features a sensitive digital tuner, alarm clock, sleep timer, and built-in charger for NiMH/NiCAD batteries. Perfect for a traveler who appreciates local airwaves.

The Groove Tube

www.velocityartanddesign.com

The Groove Tube is a translucent plastic box that hooks onto your television screen and turns it into a disco accessory. Its grid of dividers diffuses the colors from your TV and creates a colorful abstraction of whatever is on the air.

Business Card Scanner

www.cardscan.com

The CardScan Personal Scanning Device scans a business card and enters all the lines of info into the appropriate fields of an electronic address book.

The Beer Machine

www.cabelas.com

Here's a way they can make their own beer—then after they've brewed the first batch they get to name their brand, throw a party, and start chugging.

Underwater MP3 Player

www.waterproofmusic.com

Swimming laps takes on a whole new rhythm with the Finis SwimP3 Waterproof MP3 player.

Binoculars/Digital Camera

www.telescopes.com

When a regular zoom isn't enough, a binocular camera should get the job done. Celestron's VistaPix 3.1 has 8× magnification and can download images to a computer easily.

The Everything Watch

www.altrec.com

Ideal for outdoors, the Suunto X6HRM is a heart rate monitor, altimeter, compass, barometer, and thermometer watch.

Scrolling LED Badge

www.thinkgeek.com

No more "Hello My Name Is . . ." This customizable name badge with scrolling LED message can display up to six messages.

Personal Home Audio Tap

www.spyworld.com

The Tele-Monitor 2000 audio monitor lets you remotely listen in on what's happening back home by tapping into a preset device that plugs into a regular phone jack. Just call from any normal telephone line and listen—it won't affect any incoming or outgoing calls.

Electric Scooter

www.sd-electric-scooters.com

The Badsey Racer is eco-friendly and a good time. Charge it up and zip off.

The Super Ear

www.spyworld.com

Works like binoculars, but for your ears. This sound enhancer comes with earphones and lets you listen in on quiet and private conversations.

Heated Keyboard

www.cyberguys.com

It's not easy to type when your fingers are frozen! This Warmkeyboard Heated USB Keyboard solves that problem by keeping your digits warmed. Heating elements underneath the keys radiate heat into your hands. Standard 104-key layout.

TV Microscope

www.x-tremegeek.com

This high-resolution portable digital microscope allows you to get an up close and personal look at *anything*. Its 100× magnification with built-in illuminator provides richly detailed video of the item and displays the image directly onto your TV screen.

Light-Up Slippers

www.x-tremegeek.com

The Brightfeet Lighted Slippers are able to sense when you are standing in them in the dark, and the toes will light up with LED bulbs to illuminate a path.

Refrigerator Air Purifier

www.cozydays.com

The IonizAir Refrigerator Air Purifier keeps a fridge fresh and food purified. This battery-operated device will eliminate food odors in the fridge, reduce food spoilage, and even sterilize a fridge once an hour: 4½" × 2½" × 2¾".

Wireless Hotspot Finder

www.walmart.com 🎁

If they have wi-fi on their computer, the convenient IOGEAR WiFi HotSpots Explorer will help them find a zone. Push a button, the LED lights indicate a scan, and stay on once they find a hot spot. Gadget is small enough to use as a key ring.

Color Monitor Calibrator

www.pantone.com 🎁🎁🎁

If they're into printing digital photos off their computer, this color monitor calibrator will make sure that the colors seen on their monitor match the colors in the printed photos. The Pantone "Huey" Color Control Program is easy to use and is a must for anyone who counts on quality color printing.

Waterproof SLR Camera Case

www.thewaterproofstore.com 🎁🎁🎁

The SLR Camera Case from Aquapac gives you the power to take photos underwater with your SLR camera. The case is waterproof up to fifteen feet and also protects a camera from the elements. It holds SLR cameras up to 6" wide and 4" high, and will support lenses up to 3.2" long and 3" in diameter.

USB Computer Light

www.shiptheweb.com 🎁

This nifty Kikkerland LED light plugs into a computer's USB port to shine a light on your work.

Mathmos Projector

www.zincdetails.com 🎁🎁🎁

The Mathmos Projector casts a colorful moving image of up to 1.5 m onto walls, ceilings, or water. It's good for creating a loungy mood at a party. Projector is silver and comes with choice of red/blue or blue/green color wheel.

The Cable Turtle

www.themut.com 🎁

This gadget keeps extraneous cables tucked away with the turn of a hand.

Tempo Time Tag

www.vessel-store.com 🎁/two tags

These tiny digital clocks are only an inch long and clip onto anything. Made of stainless steel, each runs on a lithium battery.

Guardian Portable Night-Light

www.vessel-store.com 🎁🎁

The portable lantern hangs on a plug-in unit that glows and magnetically charges the lantern. When the lantern is removed from the charge, it lights up and provides up to five hours of night light.

Electric Dice Set

www.karmakiss.com

Roll these two balls and they beep while dots flash and light up to tell you what your number is.

Luke Skywalker's Force FX Lightsaber Ep. VI

www.masterreplicas.com

For die-hard Star Wars fans, this official reproduction of Luke's Lightsaber from *Star Wars: Episode VI: Return of the Jedi* will thrill. The glowing, bright green blade ignites with realistic power-up and power-down lights effects. The authentic Lightsaber sound effects are digitally recorded from the movie and are motion sensor controlled.

Swimming Pool Radio

www.smarthome.com

Pools parties have a whole new vibe with this radio that transmits music above and below the water.

THE ANGST-RIDDEN TEEN

Everything is embarrassing to the angst-ridden teen. Getting picked up from parties by Mom and Dad. Being ordered to babysit younger siblings on their first days in high school. And sweating through the pressures of teen love—remember the trauma of your first real kiss? Exactly—it looked a lot less sloppy in the movies.

The awkward teen is as American as Clearasil, and they'll do whatever they can to duck out of life as they know it. That's where you can lend a hand. Since they're usually strapped for cash, angst-ridden teens welcome outside contributions to support their latest disappearing act. Help them tune out their world with bass-pumping headphones, or vanish into the hottest video-game fantasy on their Sony PlayStation, or zip off to a friend's house on a tricked-out electric skateboard so they can dodge answering "How was your day?" on that particular day. As frustrating and difficult as it is to deal with this species, think back to your own pain—the daily wardrobe anguish, hormonal imbalance, wicked teachers—and let them suffer in peace. They'll thank you later . . . much later . . . when it's cool to like their family again.

Punching Bag

www.everlastboxing.com 🎁🎁🎁🎁

Here's something they can work out their angst on: the Everlast Freestanding Heavy Bag punching bag. After a tough day at school, it's better than beating up the bully.

Radar Gun

www.opticsplanet.net 🎁🎁🎁

Pull out a lawn chair on the front lawn and track your speedy neighbors whizzing by with a Bushnell Velocity Speed Gun. Also good for clocking pets and baseballs.

Snowy Boogie Board

www.backcountry.com 🎁🎁🎁🎁

Blow up an inflatable Airboard Freeride, hit the snowy slopes, and fly down the mountain on your belly. It's like a boogie board, but cold.

Ion Audio DJ Turntable Kit

www.ionaudio.com 🎁🎁🎁🎁

The iDJ03 Direct-Drive DJ Turntable Kit comes with two aluminum direct-drive turntables, headphones, cartridges, mic, and two-channel mixer.

iPod Stereo Bag

www.drbott.com 🎁🎁🎁

The Techwiz Innovations Musak Laptop Bag is not just a functional computer bag. Plug an iPod into the built-in speakers, and you've got a portable and functional stereo.

Memorex Portable Karaoke Machine

www.target.com 🎁🎁

Compact and light, the lyrics pop up on this karaoke machine's monitor. It also has enhanced vocal effects and dual microphone inputs for duets.

MTV Logo Pillow

http://shop.mtv.com 🎁🎁

Own a piece of pop culture. They can rest easy on this MTV logo pillow.

Sony PlayStation Portable

www.bestbuy.com 🎁🎁🎁🎁

The Sony PSP offers more than video games with amazing graphics on a wide-screen LCD. It's wireless and will play movies and music.

Custom-Designed Ultrasuede Guitar Strap

www.builtbywendy.com 🎁🎁

The budding rocker will love a personalized guitar strap. Just send in three photographs, and they'll be sewn into the strap. Seven strap colors available.

DJ Academy

www.scratch.com 🎁🎁🎁🎁/beginner's course

They can learn how to mix and scratch like a pro at the Scratch DJ Academy in NYC or L.A. Jam Master J is one of the founders. Equipment is provided.

Musical Instrument

www.samash.com prices vary

Help them realize their musical potential. Sam Ash carries

any musical instrument you could imagine. Pair it with a music lesson with a professional instructor, and you may help create a band.

Automatic Skateboard

www.wheelmanup.com 🎁🎁🎁🎁🎁

It moves like a surfboard or skateboard, only the Wheelman's speed is controlled by a handheld pneumatic ball. The motor and frame are supported at each end by a spokeless wheel.

Hummer CD Player/Clock Radio

www.hummerstuff.com 🎁🎁🎁

The rugged scale-model HUMMER H2 features include CD drive hidden in the roof, controls hidden under the hood, four speakers hidden in the wheels, remote control, clock/radio with alarm and snooze controls, working headlights and taillights that indicate power on and an AM/FM stereo tuner with twenty presets.

Scarface Action Figure with Sounds

www.mezcotoyz.com 🎁

Al Pacino looks like he can still kick some ass . . . even as a 10"-high action figure. Press a button and hear nine different sound clips, including: "Say hello to my little friend" and "I'm Tony Montana."

iPod Nano Clip

www.acmemade.com 🎁🎁

This high-quality leather iPod nano case protects the device and can conveniently clip onto anything with its brushed stainless steel metal clip. Comes in black or orange.

Cool Winter Sled

www.3playinc.com 🎁🎁🎁

Why send your kids down a snowy hill on a garbage pail top? Make sure they're the coolest on the hill with a rad sled, the Snow Car 4x4. Wide-track four-ski steering, a stainless center-mount lever brake, padded seats, and room for two.

Video Game Service

www.gamefly.com 🎁+/month

Like Netflix but for video games—choose from over 2,000 titles for PlayStation 2, Xbox, GameCube, and Game Boy Advanced. No due dates, no late fees; return used games for a new round of fun.

Revenge CD and Earplugs

www.wishingfish.com 🎁

It's a great way to annoy their buddies, but you might want to request they don't use this at home. The CD features twenty annoying sound effect tracks, including: Drill, Party (At Least 200 People), Drum, High Heels, Doors Banging, Bowling, and Newborn Baby.

Customized Rubik's Cube

www.personalcreations.com 🎁

Send in six favorite photos, and they'll be printed on each side of a Rubik's Cube. It's long-term distraction.

Designer Color iPod Nano

www.colorwarepc.com 🎁🎁🎁🎁

Thought you were limited to black-and-white when it

comes to a nano? How about one in metallic purple, red, or blue? Colorware likes turning electronics into custom-colored works of art, including nanos in your choice of over twenty vibrant shades. Select a color for the body and another color for the wheel, and you've got a customized gadget.

Digital Pocket Photo Album

www.target.com 🎁🎁🎁

This tiny MAGPIX Titanium Silver Digital Pocket Photo Album has a bright 1.5" LCD screen and an internal 16MB memory so they can carry tons of images around—literally in their pocket. Device comes with a USB cable and necessary software to organize and transfer photos.

Video Game Chair

www.everythingfurniture.com 🎁🎁🎁

They can play video games in ultimate style in a specially designed ergonomic video game chair.

Sunglasses

www.sunglasshut.com prices vary

All cool kids need a pair of sunglasses—but don't you try to pick out the style they'd want. Give them a gift card for a pair and let them do the choosing. Cards come in increments of $25 and are redeemable at all U.S. Sunglass Hut retailers.

Customized Converse Sneakers

www.converse.com 🎁🎁

Give a gift card good for a "Converse One, Design Your

Own Shoe Experience" and some lucky person will get to design a one-of-a-kind pair of Chuck Taylor slip canvas shoes. They choose the color of the exterior parts, the interior, the rubber siding and the stitching, top it off with a special name or message, and the shoes will arrive in about three to four weeks.

SwissMemory 1GB Alox

www.swissknivesexpress.com

The New SwissMemory Alox is a standard Swiss Army Knife with scratch-resistant anodized aluminum sides and the usual blade, file, screwdriver, scissors, and key ring. But this new model now includes a USB 1GB removable memory stick.

Zeno Acne Clearing Device

www.beautyexclusive.com

Here's a nonmedicinal way to zap zits. Zeno is a clinically proven medical heat dose treatment device intended for the treatment of individual acne pimples in people with mild to moderate acne. The treatment packages contains the Zeno Clearing Device, treatment tip cartridge, a wall charging plug, and instructions.

Scrolling LED Belt Buckle

www.scrollingbeltbuckle.com

This battery-operated belt buckle can store up to six scrolling messages at a time—each message can contain up to 256 characters. The actual belt is not included, but the buckle is compatible with any belt they may already have. Batteries are included.

Bose SoundDock for iPod

http://store.apple.com 🎁🎁🎁🎁

Everyone wants one of these. With the Bose SoundDock Digital Music System, you can listen to an iPod in Bose stereo quality. Charges the iPod while docked.

Build-Your-Own Messenger Bag

www.timbuk2.com 🎁🎁+

Create a personalized Timbuk 2 messenger bag. Just select the size, color combination, and accessory details, and you've got a specialty bag ready to roll.

Yuck! The Encyclopedia of Everything Nasty Book

www.amazon.com 🎁

Somebody had to do it. This guide details everything most people find disgusting—from the science behind burps and eye gunk to maggots and lice to cannibals and toilets.

Doodle Therapy

www.patinastores.com 🎁

What would Freud say? They can analyze the meaning behind their doodles and yours with this set of twenty-five doodle decoder cards.

PSP Case

www.kolobags.com 🎁🎁

Store a PSP in an urban camouflage case. It has space for the PSP itself plus pockets for ear buds and discs.

Numark iPod Mixing Station

http://store.apple.com

iPods have officially taken over the universe—and now they can be used to DJ. The Numark iDJ Mixing Station has inputs for two iPods, a microphone, three-band EQ, USB connectors for each iPod, inputs for additional equipment, plus lots more.

Translucent Skull

www.capricornslair.com

At five inches tall and six inches from front to back, this clear resin skull is highly detailed and distinctively creepy.

Noise-Canceling Headphones

www.bose.com

The premium Bose Quiet Comfort 2 Acoustic Noise Canceling Headphones improve the quality of the music and sounds that they want to hear, and cancel out the noises that they don't. They're ergonomically designed, lightweight, and fold flat for easy packing.

Lomographic Fish-Eye Camera

http://shop.lomography.com/shop

This is the world's only 35 mm camera that has a built-in fish-eye lens, so the pictures are distorted to look like they were taken through a peephole in a door. Since it's regular 35 mm film, the images can be developed anywhere.

Remote Control Hand

www.thingsyouneverknew.com

Unsuspecting victims get flipped off by a realistic remote

control hand that lifts its middle finger. Hand works from up to fifty feet away.

Whatever Clock

www.ournameismud.com

Ceramic white square clock where the numbers have "fallen" to the bottom and it has "Whatever" written across it: 7.25" × 7.25".

THE HOLLYWOOD HOUND

A product of the modern world, the Hollywood Hound is a delusional beast living in an altered state of reality. It's a world where their best buds are Madonna and Denzel and where their surroundings are cluttered with framed movie posters, celebrity bobbleheads, and alphabetically filed DVDs. While you may think they have more tinsletown tidbits than they could possibly need, rest assured there's always room for more. *More* exclusive VIP autographs. *More* enhanced movie watching experiences. Even *more* opportunities to turn themselves into Hollywood stars. Who knows? Maybe you'll be the one who finally pushed them into writing their own Oscar-worthy screenplay. It's difficult for the Hounds to accept the ordinary world when the glamour of Hollywood keeps calling their names. So maybe it's time to just embrace their fantasy existence and consider yourself a special guest star.

Personalized Walk of Fame Star

www.giftoffame.com 🎁🎁

These Hollywood Walk of Fame star replicas are made by the same artist who creates the plaques given to the celebrities when they receive a star on the sidewalk! Have a star like those on the Walk of Fame in Hollywood, with a special person's name on it. All hand-painted stars are nicely framed and come with a certificate of authenticity. They measure 16" × 16" and weigh under two pounds.

Original Movie Poster One-Sheets

www.moviepostershop.com 🎁+

If you know someone's favorite movie, or if there's a movie that has some special significance to your relationship, you can probably find a poster for it here. The older it is, the less likely there will be an original, but reproductions are available, too.

Personalized DVD Movie Night Intro

www.htmarket.com 🎁🎁🎁🎁

Start a movie night with an exclusive trailer that features fifteen minutes of trivia and then a customized trailer welcoming viewers to your personal home theater.

TiVo

www.tivo.com 🎁🎁🎁🎁 + monthly subscription cost

Never miss a program again with the TiVo DVR. Comes with varying sizes of memory.

Movie Star Paper Dolls

www.tomtierney.com 🎁

Not your ordinary paper dolls, these are drawn by a fashion

illustrator and come with lots of options. Themed books feature stars from across the decades, including *Glamorous Movie Stars of the Thirties Paper Dolls* with Clark Gable, Joan Crawford, and Judy Garland.

Director's Label Series Boxed Set

www.amazon.com

This DVD set features the complete music video catalogs of some of the most inventive directors, the Works of Spike Jonze, Michel Gondry, and Chris Cunningham. The set comes with the three Director's Label DVDs and each accompanying fifty-two-page booklet, plus a bonus fourth DVD featuring some of their new works and conversations.

Personalized Director's Chair

www.teamlogo.com

This 18" table-height director's chair is custom embroidered with a name, and you can select your wood color, canvas color, print color, and font.

Bates Motel Key Chain

www.shopexit9.com

For "psycho" friends, this key chain looks like an authentic vintage motel key . . . Use with caution.

Final Draft 7 Scriptwriting Program

www.amazon.com

So maybe they decide it's time to create their own little bit of Hollywood. Final Draft is a program that will help them put together an original script.

Death Certificates

www.citymorguegiftshop.com 🎁

You'll find many death certificates of the legends, including Ronald Reagan, Jerry Garcia, and Kurt Cobain. These items make the perfect gift for someone with a sick fascination with Hollywood.

Vintage Movie Posters

www.filmposters.com 🎁🎁+

It's the reel deal: authentic, original movie posters. These advertisements were produced in limited quantities and displayed in theaters when the film was first released.

Show Swag

www.hbo.com 🎁🎁 for *Sopranos* robe

For those with favorite TV shows, you can always go to the network's site and get them some cool gear. *Sopranos* fans would kill for a Tony Soprano–endorsed bathrobe.

Netflix Subscription

www.netflix.com 🎁/month

You can enjoy this with them . . . unlimited movie rentals on a monthly basis.

Old-Fashioned Popcorn Maker

www.snappypopcorn.com 🎁🎁🎁🎁+

Movie theater popcorn at home automatically makes the movie much more fun to watch.

Celebrity Autographs

http://autographsforsale.com 🎁+

Authentic signed photographs, clothing, and collectibles

of your favorite celebrities from sports, music, movies, television, politics, and fashion.

Tickets to Television Tapings

www.tvtickets.com or www.hollywoodtickets.com prices vary

If you're ever out in L.A., there are lots of ways to get free tix to a wide selection of show tapings.

Luxurious Home Theater Seating

www.htmarket.com 🎁🎁🎁🎁🎁

The Pinnacle Lounger, a two-person leather cinema-style lounger, will go perfectly with the homemade movie theater–style popcorn.

Digital Video Camera

www.bestbuy.com 🎁🎁🎁🎁+

They want to make movies? They need to start with a camera. Your options are as big as your wallet; low-end digital cameras will cost several hundred dollars, while high-end, broadcast/film-quality cameras will range in the thousands.

Premiere Magazine

www.premiere.com 🎁/two-year subscription

Get the inside scoop on the movie biz with a subscription to *Premiere* magazine. The rag has all the latest dirt on the A-listers, films in production, and up-to-the-minute news on what's happening in the business.

Authentic Memorabilia

www.gottahaveit.com 🎁+

Gotta Have It is the premier resource for the highest quality collectibles and memorabilia. The company has earned a reputation for fully authenticated sports, entertainment, and historical memorabilia. They've partnered with Sotheby's for online auctions, as well as the Juvenile Diabetes Research Fund, the Hard Rock Café, and VH1's Save the Music, to name a few. You can purchase anything from a Robert De Niro signed *Taxi Driver* photograph ($600) to an Aerosmith signed electric guitar ($2,900) to Jim Nabors's *Gomer Pyle* original shirt ($4,500).

Classic Movie Plates

www.bettysattic.com

This set of four porcelain 8" dessert plates features vintage poster artwork from *The Wizard of Oz* (1939), *King Kong* (1933), *Casablanca* (1942), and *Gone with the Wind* (1939). Microwave and dishwasher safe.

Screen Gems Gift Basket

www.gothambaskets.com

Spice up the movie fan's palate with the Screen Gems gift basket from Gotham Baskets. Contained in a large acrylic theater-style movie bucket are Real Theater Popcorn, movie candy favorites, Movie Trivia Fortune Cookies, Video Munchies popcorn, snack mix, movie trivia playing cards, popcorn jelly beans, the Quizmo! Movie Trivia Game, and a Chocolate Movie Award.

Gourmet Popcorn Gift Tin

www.daleandthomaspopcorn.com

Next time they settle in to watch another movie, treat them to some out-of-the-ordinary popcorn to go with it. The 6.5-gallon Dale and Thomas Popcorn Gift Tin can be filled with classic popcorn or with a gourmet combination. Some interesting options are Peanut Butter with White Chocolate Drizzle, Twice as Nice Drizzle, and Toffee Crunch Drizzle.

Customized Superstar Bio Video

www.funnybitstudios.com 🎁🎁🎁

The *Hollywood Spotlight* humorous fake biography portrays someone you know as a chart-topping pop music star or a glamorous movie star. Each video runs about ten minutes and uses photographs you submit to tell the story of their rise to fame. The DVD also features a DVD menu and video photo album, along with a personalized message by you to close it.

Leonard Maltin's Movie Guide 2006

http://us.penguingroup.com 🎁

Every movie lover needs this comprehensive film guide!

Leonard Maltin's Movie Encyclopedia

http://us.penuingroup.com 🎁

This bible features career profiles of more than 2,000 actors and filmmakers, past and present.

Authentic Movie Script

www.hollywoodbookandposter.com 🎁/script

Since 1977, Hollywood Book and Poster has been selling movie posters, photographs, and scripts of the biggest and best movies and TV shows ever made. They have scripts of everything from *Gone with the Wind* to *Valley of the Dolls* to recent films like *Walk the Line.*

Clapboard Tote Bag

www.hollywoodmegastore.com

They can feel like a real Hollywood type carrying this tote made to look like a film clapper. Measures 19" × 18" and is made of durable fabric.

Personalized Oscar

www.hollywoodmegastore.com

Your pal will feel like a superstar when he receives his Oscar. This 11" gold plastic statue looks just like the real guy, and you can personalize the name plate with a message up to three lines.

American Idol Audition Book and CD

www.amazon.com

This AI audition book has eighteen classic songs, with a backtrack CD for accompaniment. Start practicing!

Sundance Film Collection

www.sundancechannelstore.com

This set of ten films includes a range of dramas and documentaries. Some of the titles included are *sex, lies and videotape*, *Clerks*, *The Usual Suspects*, and *American Movie*. Also comes with a bonus disc that features behind-the-scenes info on Sundance and an interview with Robert Redford.

THE KNOW-IT-ALL

You know this person: that friend who's always right because she "read it in the *Times*" last week. The cousin who frequently challenges you to games he's good at simply because he loves to win. The colleague who thinks it's impressive to prattle off obscure references he knows no one will ever get. You've probably had to deal with a Know-It-All, and it's never an easy job. Every exchange is a challenge, every subject fair game. And while the Know-It-All may be full of information that's useful—even interesting—most of the time, you could have gone without. It's a tough task getting something for the person who knows it all. Start by pinpointing a subject they know nothing about, and then give them the tools they need to crack the subject: ancient Rome . . . linguistics . . . yoga! Introduce them to a brand-new game no one's ever played. Or better yet, acquaint them with something *you* know a lot about, so when the topic comes back to haunt you, you've wisely evened the know-it-all playing field. Then gloat.

Pirate Booty

www.atocha1622.com 🎁🎁🎁🎁+

You can purchase an actual coin from the Spanish treasure ship *Nuestra Senora de Atocha*, which sunk in 1622 off the Florida coast. The wreck of the *Atocha* and her lode of silver, gold, and emeralds were located in 1985. Each item comes with a certificate of authenticity.

Trivial Pursuit

www.hasbrotoyshop.com 🎁🎁

Now they can kick your butt in this game, too! Get them the latest edition of Trivial Pursuit.

Paint-By-Numbers Art

www.weegohome.com 🎁🎁🎁🎁

It's all there for assembly: stretcher frame, canvas with pre-drawn design, acrylic paints, and brushes. Choose between 32" square or 40" square sizes.

Lomography Colorsplash Camera

http://shop.lomography.com/shop 🎁🎁

This cool camera has a flash with a color wheel to throw red, blue, green, or yellow light on the scene.

Urban Myth Game

www.uncommongoods.com 🎁🎁

How much do they really know? This game challenges you to separate fact from fiction as it questions 1,100 myths in six categories (Celebrity, Crime, Nature, Health, Business, and Classics).

Yoga Deluxe Journey Kit

www.huggermugger.com 🎁🎁🎁

Do they know the difference between an up dog and a cobra? Time they learned. This beginner's kit comes with a bag, mat, block, belt, and an instructional DVD.

Courses

www.teach12.com 🎁🎁+

Join in on an actual course taught by a college professor. These series of lectures cover everything from the Life and Writings of C. S. Lewis to the Ethics of Aristotle to Bach and the High Baroque. Lessons available on videotape, CD, or audiotape.

Framed Stamp Art

www.brownson5th.com 🎁🎁

Over 100 choices of canceled stamp art professionally mounted and framed. Choose from a wide range of subjects such as Professions, the Arts, and Birds and Animals.

Mensa Games

www.mensaboutique.com 🎁+

Do they have the brains for Mensa? Choose from a number of board and card games that challenge the mind and test a person's smarts.

Learn to Sail

www.ussailing.org prices vary

Here's a sport that takes focus and precision. There are hundreds of facilities where you can learn to sail on a variety of vessels. This website will help you pinpoint a location and a school.

Art Books

www.artbook.com prices vary

D.A.P. (Distributed Art Publishers) boasts a huge up-to-date selection of books, special editions, and rare publications from the best international publishers, museums, and cultural institutions worldwide. High-quality books cover subjects like art, photography, architecture, design, fashion, and culture.

Rare Book

www.manhattanrarebooks.com 🎁🎁🎁🎁+

If they like to read, this will make them appreciate a good book. The Manhattan Rare Book Company specializes in outstanding rare books in excellent condition.

Bird-Watching Book

www.nationalgeographic.com 🎁

For the future bird-watching expert, get them started with the indispensable *National Geographic Field Guide to the Birds of North America.* This ultimate birding resource includes all known North American species.

Ship-in-a-Bottle Kit

www.nauticalsupplyshop.com 🎁

These ship-in-a-bottle kits will reveal the secrets of getting a ship into a bottle. Choose from a number of different ship models.

Personal Jigsaw Puzzle

www.portraitpuzzles.com 🎁+

Challenge them to complete a high-quality jigsaw puzzle

featuring a favorite photograph. Puzzles can contain as few as 48 pieces and as many as 756.

Book-of-the-Month Club

www.bookswithbows.com 🎁🎁🎁🎁/year

Packages available include one where each month, you receive the latest hardcover edition of the current bestselling fiction. Packages also available for know-it-all kids.

Make Your Own Sushi Kit

www.cooking.com 🎁🎁

This make your own sushi kit comes with everything they'd need to learn the craft: cookbook, short-grain rice, nori for wrapping the sushi, pickled ginger, spicy wasabi horseradish, dark soy sauce, rice vinegar, sushi vinegar, rice paddle, and bamboo mat for rolling up the final product.

History of Home

www.loc.gov prices vary

The United States Library of Congress carries antique maps of cities and sites across America. For a New Yorker, there's nothing like a vintage map of Manhattan dating back to 1872.

Gourmet Movie Membership

www.nicheflix.com 🎁+

It's Netflix with foreign and indie films for the discerning movie watcher. Select from among cult TV, anime, Eurocinema, horror, and more.

Old Guns

www.casiberia.com 🎁+

History buffs can enjoy a replica of a historical weapon. One item available is an exact (nonfireable) replica of the most used revolver in the Civil War, the M1860 percussion revolver purchased by the Union Army.

NYT Electronic Crossword Puzzle

www.hammacherschlemmer.com 🎁🎁🎁

The *New York Times* handheld electronic crossword puzzle contains 1,000 puzzles from the *Times* archive for endless challenges.

Oxford English Dictionary Online

www.oed.com 🎁🎁🎁🎁/year

Buy them an annual membership to the *OED* Online, and they'll have access to the twenty-volume second edition, plus three additional volumes. They'll find pronunciations, etymologies, quotations from specified years or authors/works, plus more, using a number of sophisticated searching options.

Albert Einstein Action Hero

www.thinkgeek.com 🎁

Go, Einstein, go! If anything will remind a genius of his own limitations, it's an Einstein action figure. Your friend may be smart, but are they as smart as *Time* magazine's Person of the Century? The hard vinyl Albert Einstein action figure measures 5½".

Sony Voice Recorder

www.sonystyle.com 🎁🎁🎁🎁

So they can keep track of all their genius thoughts. The ICD-SX25VTP voice recorder comes with software that allows them to translate from voice to text on the computer so they can put together their brilliant thoughts. Stores over eleven hours of recordings.

Gigantic Jigsaw

www.puzzlesusa.com 🎁🎁🎁

Stick it to them with this 9,000-piece jigsaw puzzle of an ornate and highly detailed antique world map.

Parlor Puzzles Collection Set

www.parlorpuzzles.com 🎁🎁

Here are eight ways to bend their brain. The entire collection of Parlor Puzzles features metal mental challenges that will keep them busy for a long time.

NYT Electronic Trivia Quiz Game

www.nytstore.com 🎁🎁

The *New York Times* Electronic Quiz Game challenges users with multiple-choice questions in themed groups of eight by noted trivia master Ray Hamel. Can be played alone or as a game with two players.

Handwriting Analysis Kit

www.powells.com 🎁

This set comes with everything they need to learn how to gain insight to a person through their handwriting. Included are a book and demonstration on how to interpret handwriting, a plastic tool that measures the details of a person's handwriting, and paper for collecting samples.

Pocket Reference Guide

www.amazon.com

This handy book covers everything you ever wanted to know and never really needed to know about everything. Subjects include topics like air and gas properties, anniversary traditions, two-letter codes for airlines, and classifications for plastic pipes.

Black Widow Brainteaser

www.gamedaze.com 

It's a mess of metal, and the goal is to remove the ball and cord from the puzzle. Good luck to them.

"Genius" Mug

www.ournameismud.com 

This sturdy ceramic mug has "Genius" hand painted across it just in case anyone was in doubt.

The Book of Useless Information

www.amazon.com 

Formed in 1995, the Useless Information Society comprises Britain's foremost thinkers, writers, and artists. If it's information not a lot of people know—and no one really needs to know—it's in here.

THE NEWBORN BABE

Today's babies have the life. They ride easy in ergonomic strollers on air bubble–filled wheels, sleep soundly in cribs with built-in fans for gentle white noise, and dine on jarred delicacies like apple mango kiwi and pasta primavera. This may all seem quite decadent, but you can have fun indulging these burgeoning princes and princesses. There are lessons to be learned with custom-made educational videotapes starring the people they know and love. Or political statements to be made on onesies that shout "Question Authority!" and "Sworn to Fun, Loyal to None." Of course, there are always tony tastes to be trained with sterling play toys from Tiffany & Co. Sure, keeping up with baby trends may be as hard as the car seats you used to ride in, but think of it this way: when these kids start working in about twenty years, you'll be thankful for your contribution to the most stylish generation in history.

Baby Tutu and Tee

www.ink-well.net 🎁🎁

Tutu and tee set includes a diaper cover, tutu, and matching soft lap T-shirt. Both items can be monogrammed with a single initial.

Cashmere Baby Blanket

www.kinder-cashmere.com 🎁🎁🎁🎁

Soft cashmere blanket with an elegant barnyard animal silhouette.

Children's Music Box

www.shopkitson.com 🎁🎁

These handmade wooden music boxes by Kerri Lee are a great keepsake. Each one plays a different song. Available in pink ("Thank Heaven for Little Girls") and Green ("Doggie in the Window").

The Original Clean Shopper Baby

www.cleanshopper.com 🎁🎁

A germ-phobic mom invented this baby protector. The 100 percent cotton one-piece design fits perfectly in most shopping carts where your tot would sit. The quilted protector keeps bacteria and germs away from your child.

Gucci Baby Carrier

www.gucci.com 🎁🎁🎁🎁🎁

BABYBJÖRN who? Gucci baby carrier comes in the classic beige and brown insignia with brown leather straps or black.

Baby Kimono

www.samandseb.com 🎁🎁

One hundred percent cotton kimono comes packaged in a sushi container.

Cool Bibs

www.sourpussclothing.com 🎁

For the rocker babies ready to give props to AC/DC and the Ramones.

Baby Perfume

www.burberry.com 🎁🎁

Burberry makes a light, sweet, hypoallergenic scent for babies called Baby Touch.

Baby Stroller

www.babystyle.com 🎁🎁🎁🎁🎁

The Stokke Xplory baby stroller brings babies' seat level up to an adult height so they can enjoy the same views. And it keeps them father away from dirt.

Sheepskin Sleeping Bag

www.vivre.com 🎁🎁🎁🎁🎁

This cozy sheepskin baby snuggle bag is machine washable and fits children six months to three years.

Daddy Belt

www.dreamtimebaby.com 🎁🎁

Is he doing work around the house or watching the baby? This dad-appropriate tool belt-ish bag has the organizational features of a diaper bag without looking girlie.

Pee-pee Teepee

www.uncommongoods.com 🎁

You'll never get sprayed again. This convenient shield keeps your baby boy from getting you wet.

Personalized Canvas Baby Rug

www.babybrowns.com

This personalized, hand painted 36" square canvas floor cover features adorable designs and can be customized with a name or birth announcement.

Bib-of-the-Month Club

www.babybrowns.com /6 mos.; /12 mos.

Bored with your bibs? Then this is the club for you! Baby Brown's Bib-of-the-Month Club sends you a new, fun, and surprising bib every month!

Personalized Baby Book

www.mamabebe.com

My Very Own Name is a professionally bound, hardcover book customized for any name. In the story, animals gather, each carrying a letter that eventually creates the baby's first and last names. Each letter is the first letter of that animal, so an association can begin for when it's time to learn to spell. Book can also include the birth date and a printed message from the person giving the book.

Personalized Baby Skullcap

www.personalizedforbaby.com

Skullcaps should do more than keep a baby's head warm—they can make fashion statements! Choose a color and custom design with baby's name.

The Complete Patemm Changing Pad

www.patemm.com

A round option to your typically square changing pad. Also doubles as a bag for diapers, wipes and clothes.

Infant Urban "Bundle Me" Sac

www.target.com 🎁🎁

This baby sac keeps the kid warm in a car seat, stroller, or jogger. It has a wind- and water-resistant exterior, a warm microfiber lining, and is available in three colors.

Professionally Painted Portrait

www.annewaybernard.com 🎁🎁🎁🎁 (11" × 14")

Capture the baby's first photo in a timeless oil painting. Anne Bernard works off photographs and will provide helpful tips on how to take the best photo for her to reproduce.

Customized Baby Videos

www.infantrecognition.com 🎁🎁

It's one-of-a-kind . . . an educational baby video made with the family's own photos.

Babyprints Wall Frame Kit

www.pearhead.com 🎁🎁

An easy-to-assemble shadow box kit displays a baby's hand- or footprint and photo in an elegant pine frame.

Outfits with Attitude

www.wrybaby.com 🎁

Funny baby clothes—try onesies that say "I Can't Read" or "Scented" or "98% Wet."

Silver Feeding Spoon

www.tiffany.com 🎁🎁🎁

Aside from being able to say their baby was born with a silver spoon in its mouth, a sterling silver feeding spoon is always an elegant keepsake. The Tiffany Farm feeding spoon has three cute farm animals on the handle and can be engraved with the baby's initials for an additional charge.

Personalized Baby Plate

www.blueberrybabies.com 🎁🎁

One day, a plate will mean something to the kid, but in the meantime these ceramic dishes personalized with name and birth date are just really cute. Select from a series of adorable animal themes.

Mini Music Boxes

www.plumparty.com 🎁🎁

Will keep them distracted and musical. Twelve different tunes play from each of the mini music boxes.

Political Tees

www.babywit.com 🎁+

For the edgier baby, T-shirts that boast "Anarchy" and "Sex, Drugs and Rock & Roll" say it for them.

Rare First-Edition Children's Book

www.storyopolis.com prices vary

A rare children's book is something to hold on to for life.

Personalized Crib Blankets

www.theredballoon.com 🎁🎁🎁

Unique and personalized crib blankets are hand stitched for durability and softness and are machine washable. Each style incorporates the baby's name.

Monogrammed Diaper Covers

www.babybox.com

It's a bum wrap. This 100 percent cotton diaper cover can be custom embroidered with a name or initial.

Animal Names Personalized Prints

www.personalizationmall.com

The Animal Names personalized prints playfully spell out the baby's name in letters shaped by different animals. Each print is matted and framed and designed in bright, fun colors.

Personalized Baby Frame

www.personalizationmall.com

The Our New Arrival custom picture frame is a high-gloss laminated wood frame with the baby's full name, birth date, and weight uniquely designed into the wood facing. You can choose between script or block lettering, in pink or blue on a white background, or the reverse with white lettering on a pink or blue background. Frame measures 8" × 10" and holds a 4" × 6" photo.

Baby Makes Three Set

www.deandeluca.com

Dean & Deluca has an upscale baby gift set of a small pewter bowl and spoon they can use or hold on to as an heirloom, along with a Dean & Deluca baby onesie and rubber ducky.

Baby Bank

www.elegantbaby.com

It's never too early to start saving. These ceramic polka-dot piggy banks come in green, pink, or blue with white polka dots.

Infant Support Pillow by Zakeez

www.zakeez.com 🎁🎁

The Zaky Infant Support Pillow looks and feels just like a human hand and is designed to physically support a child while he or she sleeps. The hand simulates the weight, size, feel, and designated scent to provide a comforting cradle for the baby. Made of 100 percent nonpilling fleece.

Billy Bob Baby Pacifier

www.thingsyouneverknew.com 🎁

It's a baby pacifier that works just fine for the kid and makes everyone else laugh. The exterior of the soother looks like a mouth with hillbilly teeth. The poor kid won't know what's so funny.

Newborn Moses Basket

www.hoohobbers.com 🎁🎁🎁

This baby basket measures 11" × 32" × 19" and holds a duvet-style insert and bumpers. Also comes with a double-sided 100 percent cotton blanket. Choose from dozens of adorable patterns.

Baby Care Kit

www.redenvelope.com 🎁

The Baby Medical Kit comes with everything a new mother needs to care for the little one. Included for the baby are medicine spoon, nasal aspirator, digital thermometer, water-filled pretzel-shaped teether, plastic-coated nail clipper, comb, and brush.

Glamorous Diaper Cake

www.magicmondays.com 🎁+

Magic Mondays is known for baking up some incredible Diaper Cakes. Shaped like a classic tiered cake, the tiers are built on a foundation of disposable diapers, and woven in are bottles, rattles, clothing, keepsakes, and toys. Choose from the simple cupcake style or the five-tiered Jumbo Cake.

Baby's First Year Frame

www.stephanbaby.net 🎁

Silver-plated or pewter photo frame has a monthly spot for a photo as the baby goes through its first year. Center spot is for baby's first birthday photo.

Personalized Embroidered Baby Pillow

www.babybox.com 🎁🎁

This personalized baby keepsake pillow is a nice accent to a new baby's room. The baby's name and birthday are embroidered on a throw pillow that comes in a selection of six designs.

Dwell Baby Bedding

www.cocoacrayon.com 🎁🎁🎁🎁/set

Ultrastylish baby bedding makes for designer dreams. Dwell Baby crib sets come in a number of exclusive patterns and designs.

Astrological Blanket

www.babybox.com 🎁🎁🎁

Each 100 percent cotton blanket features the baby's astrological sign. The 40" × 40" blanket also comes with a name tag and a sign description. Available in pink/ivory, blue/army, and mint/army.

Designer Diaper Cover

www.bumkins.com

Who wants to look at a boring white diaper anyway? With the Bumkins Diaper Cover, you can add some splash with an adorable Dr. Seuss pattern—or better yet, a foxy leopard print.

Veggie Rattles

www.blablakids.com

The 100 percent cotton knit veggie collection comes with one of each of a carrot, radish, cabbage, pea pod, and tomato.

Flatout Bear

www.peanutbutterandlili.com

Sarah Jessica Parker is a fan of this 100 percent Australian sheepskin bear. Looks and feels like a regular teddy bear—and as easy to squeeze—it's just flat!

Hugg-A-Planet

www.toyandbookstore.com

A 6" classic globe is soft and perfect for a baby to hang on to and squeeze—all while subconsciously honing geography skills.

Happy Baby Bag

www.rockcandymusic.net

Each of the Happy Baby Bags contains a themed instrumental CD and a special soft puppet. Music covers everything from James Taylor to Mozart to show tunes.

Penguin Future Reader Onesie

http://us.penguingroup.com/

It's never too early to become a book fan. The white cotton onesie has the Penguin logo and the words "Future Reader."

Baby Mailer Outfit

www.catfishgreetings.com

This 100 percent cotton long-sleeve T-shirt with leggings comes packaged in an adorable ready-to-mail box. Just add postage to the outside and drop in the mail. Choose a cute title and corresponding drawing from: peanut, honey bunny, little prince, princessa, sweet pea, and monkey.

THE CRUNCHY CONFIDANTE

Have you ever tried a kale and seaweed salad? Or grilled tofu with broccoli, chili, and lime? To some, those dishes may sound disgusting. But to the Crunchy Confidante, it sounds like lunch. These folks have stepped off the sunny peace-loving communes of the '70s and into the dizzying bustle of modern urban life. They load up their energy-conserving hybrid cars with organic groceries from farmers' markets. And since yoga classes are now as available as Starbucks coffee, they can easily find a spot to ground their chakras. The Crunchy Confidantes keep our universe balanced, and there are things they can utilize to maintain this peace. Meditation classes come in all shapes and sizes, as do the accoutrements that help make their practice more comfy. While they have embraced their own spirituality, there are still places only a psychic can reach. And they will absolutely welcome assisting a nonprofit that provides positive community services. You don't have to eat the kale, but why not help them help save the world?

Folk Art

www.indigoarts.com 🎁+

Can't afford to travel around the world? There's a way to still buy indigenous crafts from faraway lands like Africa, Asia, South America, Indonesia, and more.

Sounds of the Planet

www.shop.npr.org 🎁

Ever wonder what sand sounds like? Or the solar system? NPR's *Pulse of the Planet* CD serves up over thirty sounds from the natural world.

Door Harp

www.kokogm.com 🎁🎁+

Mount a harp on the back of your door and greet your guests with a calm musical sound. Choose from a selection of woods (walnut, mahogany, cherry, oak, padouk, and ash) with five strings.

Plant a Tree

www.treegivers.com 🎁🎁

Choose a state to plant a tree in, and the person to whom it's dedicated will get a framed certificate.

Singing Bowl Gift Set

www.dharmashop.com 🎁🎁

Meditate with the sounds from an authentic singing bowl. Set includes an 8" metal bowl, a two-piece wooden and leather striker, and a small cushion in a handmade wooden box.

Meditation Mat and Cushion

www.mountainseat.com 🎁🎁🎁🎁

They'll be able to meditate for hours in comfort on the Mountain Seat Zafu and Zabuton set. Made of viscoelastic foam and buckwheat hulls.

A Piece of the Moon

www.lunarregistry.com 🎁+

There's an acre of premium property on the Moon for sale. Buy it and you'll receive a personalized parchment deed certificate, a satellite photograph of the property, and geographic information to help locate the property (whether you're viewing it through a telescope or visiting in person).

Psychic Chart

www.sloanbella.com 🎁🎁🎁

Have their astrological birth chart created and accompanied by a reading by psychic and astrologer Sloan Bella.

Vegan Delights

www.veganessentials.com 🎁

Yummy vegan treats cover everything from Meals-in-Minutes to sweet treats like vegan marshmallows and chocolates.

Mehndi Henna Kit

www.misterart.com 🎁

Kit contains henna powder with bottle and metal applicator tip, sugar/citric solution, mordant liquid, eucalyptus oil, straight pin, toothpicks, mixing stick, cotton balls, and an instruction/design ideas sheet.

An Ecosphere

www.greenfeet.com

The Ecospheres are totally enclosed ecosystems with active microorganisms—bright red shrimp and algae—all living in filtered seawater. No cleaning, no feeding, just requires minimal care—the perfect pet!

A Gift Tree

www.ecolage.com

Buy mail-order plants to give memories that grow! The wide selection includes fragrant plants, exotic vines, evergreens, Southern trees, and more.

Healing Music Collection Gift Set

www.nipponkodo.com

The Healing Collection Music CD Series comes packaged with soft incense to burn while you meditate.

Charity Donation

www.justgive.org donations at your own discretion

You allot the amount, and the receiver can choose from a ton of charity selections.

Fortune Shakers

www.plumparty.com

Red wooden sticks list fortunes. Shake out and read!

Inner Beauty Gift Box

www.twokh.com

All of the eco-friendly products in this luxurious gift box are selected to enhance your inner and outer beauty and provide total relaxation. Package includes the book *Inner*

Beauty, a cannabis candle, a mist tea, bath oil and foam, and a wool sea sponge.

Organic PJs

www.ahappyplanet.com 🎁🎁🎁

Yummy flannel pajama bottom and top made out of 100 percent organic cotton.

Donate a Heifer

www.heifer.org prices vary

Heifer International is a charity organization that helps families around the world receive training and animal gifts that help them become self-reliant. You select an animal—they have everything from heifers ($500), water buffalos ($250), sheep ($120), a flock of geese ($20)—they even have a beehive ($30). When that animal arrives, the recipients are trained to take care of it and use its resources for their survival and income. A good dairy cow can produce four gallons of milk a day—enough for a family to drink, share, and sell. Sheep provide wool for clothes and to sell. Plus, since the recipient has agreed to pass along the offspring of their gift to another family in need, the program works to help an entire community.

Mineral of the Month Club

www.mineralofthemonthclub.org 🎁/month

A deluxe membership to the Mineral-of-the-Month Club will give them something new to study each month. Members will receive specimens between 2" × 3" and 3" × 4" in size—all suitable for display. They'll also get a presentation binder to organize and store their write-ups.

Biofield Balancing Pendant

www.discountgolfworld.com 🎁🎁🎁

Apparently, everyone has a field of energy that your body gives off. The National Institutes of Health calls it a biofield and says it is what powers our daily lives. Things like computer screens, cell phones, traffic jams, and stress all disrupt a biofield, and that leads to illness, fatigue, and general malaise. The Q-Link Pendant claims to reset a biofield using a resonant effect to retune our bodies and get them back to harmony and balance.

Blossoms All-Natural Bath Products

www.blossomsnaturalbliss.com 🎁+

Blossoms Natural Bliss products are made with no "substandard ingredients, derivatives or substitutions." Their line includes candles, soaps, bath salts, lotions, and body washes. Each item comes in four fragrances: vanilla, orange, lavender, and gardenia.

Ceramic Astrology Tiles

www.poopsies.com 🎁🎁

Each 6" × 6" wood-framed ceramic tile humorously rattles off the more brazen personality traits of each zodiac sign. All twelve signs available.

Reusable Nylon Shopping Bag

www.thecontainerstore.com 🎁

Compact shopping bag comes packed into its own little pouch. Open it up when you're ready to load it up with your goods.

Encyclopedia of Natural Medicine

www.amazon.com

Written by naturopathic doctors, this nearly 1,000-page tome focuses on improving health using nontoxic, natural substances. It includes tips on treating ailments with natural remedies, as well as overall health maintenance.

THE BIG BOSS

It doesn't matter how kind bosses may be, they radiate authority and an intimidating power. It's their boat to steer, their roost to rule. The corner office with the leather chaise and the city views so obviously belongs to them. So you may be asking yourself what your boss could possibly need. Let's cut to the chase: for the gift, you should be thinking classy but not overtly expensive . . . personal, but appropriate. McDonald's gift certificates are definitely not an option. Think about what your boss does outside the office. Do they golf? How about specialty golf balls or a designer glove? Travel a lot? Luxury travel comforts will always come in handy. If you're afraid to get too off-hours, there are always sophisticated office accessories the chief can put to good use. Deep down inside, you know your boss will be thankful that you even thought to get a gift at all. And if they aren't, what's the worse that can happen? All they can do is fire you.

Brownie Star of the Month Club

www.simplydivinebrownies.com 🎁🎁🎁+

A new flavor of delicious brownies arrives every month loaded with exotic ingredients like raspberry liqueur and Wild Turkey Bourbon and sweet potato cheesecake.

Martini Set for Two to Go

www.presentdaygifts.com 🎁🎁

Wine on a picnic? Go for the martini! Picnic at Ascot makes a convenient insulated canvas bag that's loaded with stainless steel martini accessories, two glass martini glasses, and a sleek shaker.

Tumi Tie Travel Case

www.tumi.com 🎁🎁🎁

The Napa Leather tie case makes a nice gift for a traveler who needs to keep his ties wrinkle-free.

Gourmet Pilsner Glasses

www.ritzenhoffcollection.com 🎁🎁

The Ritzenhoff Collection of pilsners is imported from Germany. Choose from over forty whimsical designs.

Leather Domino Set

www.travelsmith.com 🎁🎁

A domino set comes in an attractive brown leather case with a buckle/snap closure. Set includes a scoring pad and pen.

Space Pen

www.mossonline.com 🎁

Invented for NASA, this sleek chrome pen will write on

any surface, in any situation. Each pen is supplied with a black ink medium-point specially designed pressurized ink cartridge.

Smart Mug

www.gevalia.com 🎁🎁

Great for the drive into work, just plug this sixteen-ounce red mug into a car's cigarette lighter, and a morning cup of coffee stays hot.

Leather Stationery Box

www.danier.com 🎁

Keep stationery organized in a stylish leather stationery box. Pen, envelopes, and stationery paper included. Available in white, biscuit, and butter.

Louis Vuitton Golf Glove

www.eluxury.com 🎁🎁🎁🎁

Perforated lambskin glove with stretch textile insert and a cowhide "LV" patch. Comes as a single glove—left or right.

The Traveler Alarm Clock

www.linksoflondon.com 🎁🎁🎁

Wake up to something personal on the road. This elegant silver-plated alarm clock comes in a leather travel case in a variety of colors.

Luxury Pen

www.montblanc.com 🎁+

The Montblanc pen is a classic staple for every boss. Site will help you find the nearest retailer.

Monogrammed Gella Umbrella

www.horchow.com 🎁🎁

Personal and practical—everyone could use a monogrammed umbrella in a bright color with a single initial. Made of durable polyester with gel handle for a comfortable grip.

Fancy Chocolates

www.mrchocolate.com 🎁🎁🎁🎁/12 mos.

Le Cirque's former pastry chef Jacques Torres has a chocolate shop in Brooklyn that will ship around the United States. His chocolate-of-the-month club features a new chocolate delicacy each month; it could be a flavorful bar or chocolate-covered marshmallows or even chocolate cornflakes.

Luxurious Slippers

www.maxwellsilverny.com 🎁🎁

A comfortable boss is a happy boss. From Apartment 48, the Ciccia Bella Chinese Toaster silk slipper boots have a delicate red or lime exterior and cushy fleece lining.

Weightless Flight Training

www.spaceadventures.com 🎁🎁🎁🎁🎁/U.S. ZeroG session

FAA-approved activity offers the chance to enjoy weightlessness in each Space Adventures Zero Gravity Flight program. The daylong U.S. ZeroG program will introduce the boss to a veteran astronaut and let him experience weightlessness training by experiencing fifteen parabolas of Martian, Lunar, and zero gravity. Numerous packages available.

Museum Membership

www.lacma.org, www.moma.org, www.artic.edu prices vary

A membership to a museum in your area provides bonuses they can appreciate throughout the year, and it is tax deductible for you. Most museums have a variety of annual membership packages available, but to give you an idea, the Los Angeles County Museum of Art charges $110 for a basic package, the Museum of Modern Art in New York charges $75 for an individual membership, and at the Art Institute in Chicago, it's only $70 for an individual membership.

Travel Photo Compact

www.tanthony.com 🎁🎁

Leather photo compact for the traveler in calfskin holds eighteen photos. Monogramming is available; choice of six colors.

Crystal Decanter

www.gearys.com 🎁🎁🎁

Stick with a classic from Geary's of Beverly Hills. The gorgeous Country Magnum crystal decanter has a clean, minimalist design.

Leather Card Case

www.danier.com 🎁

Playing cards are kept together in this stylish black leather case.

Elegant Travel Bath Set

www.hsnv.com 🎁🎁

Help them feel pampered while on the road for work with a Body Wash Travel Pack from Health Spa Napa Valley.

Monogrammed Golf Balls

www.redenvelope.com 🎁🎁/dozen

A dozen monogrammed Wilson Ultra Mega Distance balls are branded without impacting the balls' spin or flight.

Boxed in Blooms

www.jane-carroll.com 🎁🎁🎁+

Jane Carroll has become famous for her unique and special floral arrangements. A favorite is a classic handmade wooden box with an antique finish, filled with an arrangement of fresh-cut flowers. Available in small, medium, and large.

Cigars

www.thecigarstore.com 🎁🎁+

A strong gesture—just make sure they smoke!

Laptop Privacy Screen

www.compusa.com 🎁🎁

The Laptop LCD privacy screen slips over a laptop monitor and narrows the viewing area so that only the person directly in front of the monitor can see what's on the screen.

Financial Advisor Ball

www.kopes.com 🎁

May help lighten the mood in the office. Shake this green plastic ball, and the answers to all monetary dilemmas appear within seconds in the green window. Try for twenty different responses.

Desktop Mug Warmer

www.tabletools.com 🎁

The Salton Hot Spot Desktop Mug Warmer keeps a cup of coffee hot when they have to run into a meeting. Comes with a small warming plate and twelve-ounce mug.

Leather Pen Case

www.worldlux.com 🎁🎁

The sturdy Aston Pen Case protects luxury pens in a fine leather holder. Has slots for up to four pens and comes in tan or brown.

Portable Executive Golf Set

www.designstore.com 🎁🎁🎁

Inside the Lexon Studio–designed durable carrying case are a collapsible aluminum putter, an aluminum target hole, and two bright orange golf balls. Makes it easy for them to perfect their putt no matter where they are.

Cigar Ashtray

www.worldlux.com 🎁🎁🎁🎁

This S.T. Dupont Palladium Cigar Ashtray is designed to conveniently hold two cigars.

Electronic Tie Rack

www.sharperimage.com 🎁🎁

The PowerTie Motorized Tie Rack holds up to seventy-two ties while taking up only nine inches of a closet rod. There's even a light that automatically illuminates so it's easier to see the ties.

Hermès Scarf

www.hermes.com 🎁🎁🎁🎁

The Hermès silk twill scarf is an elegant and classic gift for her. Choose one in their signature orange.

THE CURIOUS KID

When you were a kid, there were only three television networks and remote controls weighed ten pounds. Nowadays, even a two-year-old can TiVo past commercials. When you were a kid, art class involved your fingers and paint. Today, kids create digital masterpieces in their computer literacy classes. What happened? And when? It seems that overnight, a kid's life has gotten way more complex than the days when video games featured a frog trying to cross the road. Fortunately, the basics remain; children still like to experiment with their imagination, whether it's designing an original costume or staging their own Broadway production. They still want to explore newly discovered talents like building a car or solving a mystery. And they'll always need to feel special, like when they see their name stamped across something cool. The world will continue changing, and kids will keep right in stride, but for those of you feeling left behind, Toys "R" Us will always be there.

Personalized Sleeping Bag

www.fantasytoyland.com 🎁🎁

Slumber parties are more fun in a colorful sleeping bag with your own name printed all the way down it. Bag is kid-sized at 30" × 64" and is machine washable.

Global Gifts

www.justglobes.com 🎁🎁🎁

The Leapfrog Odyssey III electronic educational globe teaches kids about the world when they touch the pen to the globe. Learn about oceans, continents, languages, and more.

Fuzzy Animal Slippers

www.onlyslippers.com 🎁🎁

Kids love slipping their feet into these friendly slippers. Choose from over a dozen options, including bunnies, puppies, and moose.

Kid's Fireman Suit

www.usillygoose.com 🎁🎁

Hard helmet, bib overalls, and fire coat—everything a kid needs to be a hero.

Band in a Box

www.ourgreenhouse.com 🎁

Everyone else in the house might not appreciate it, but the kid sure will. The ten-piece band includes tambourine, maracas, triangle, and cymbals.

Kids' Personalized Basic Towel Set

www.potterybarnkids.com 🎁🎁

Pottery Barn Kids' three-piece basic towel set comes with a bath towel, hand towel, and washcloth and can be personalized with a child's name. Towels come in a range of bright colors.

Fruity Beanbag

www.thisisauto.com 🎁🎁🎁🎁

Comfy and cute, these Eazy Bean Fruit Beanbag Chairs look like a sweet piece of fruit. Choose from a pear, orange, blueberry, lemon, gridberry, apple, or peach.

Personalized Kids' Throw Pillows

www.rumaku.com 🎁

They'll feel special with a cute throw pillow with their name on it.

Play Volcano

www.samandseb.com 🎁

Who needs science class? With a complete kit for building and erupting your own volcano, kids can make history in their own backyards.

Tattoo Dining Set

www.sourpussclothing.com 🎁

The kid can eat like a real punk—a plate featuring a Mom and Dad tattoo, complemented with a sparrow bowl and nautical star fork and spoons.

Custom-Made Soap Kits

www.brambleberry.com 🎁+

Kids can build their own custom soap kit from a selection of bases, fragrances, oils, and sizes.

Kid's Art Bag

www.bagettes.com

Turn a child's art into a one-of-a-kind bag. Just e-mail or mail in the masterpiece, and it's sent back turned into a portable canvas bag.

Starter Artist Set

www.dickblick.com

For the future Picassos, Walter Foster Sets provide everything needed to get going. Kits include paints, brushes, paper or canvas, and other tools unique to each medium. Also comes with project books with step-by-step illustrations, instructions, and lessons. Select from acrylic, oil, watercolor, or Chinese brush painting sets.

Armand Diradourian Cashmere Teddy Bear

www.thisisauto.com

These luxurious and classic bears are soft, plush, and available in five brilliant colors.

Harley-Davidson Rocker

www.dreamtimebaby.com

Because they're too young for the real deal.

Cool Lunch Pack

www.babyoliver.com

The Fleurville Lunch Pak is perfect for carrying lunch to school and projects home. Designed for three- to six-year-olds with large, soft, easy-to-use zipper pulls and bright color combinations.

Kids' Camping Set

www.summitcampinggear.com 🎁🎁

The Coleman for Kids Frontier Camping Combo includes a tent, sleeping bag, day pack, and a Coleman sport bottle. Everything they need for camping out.

Birthday Cake Plate

www.warmbiscuit.com 🎁🎁

It's one of those annual traditions. Every birthday, your child can look forward to eating cake off one of these only-for-them, hand-painted cake plates wishing them a happy birthday.

Personalized Kid CD

www.lullabiesforbabies.com 🎁

With the Deluxe CD Package, a child will get a personalized music CD with the child's name sung forty to fifty times. It comes with a lyric booklet with the child's name printed on the cover and the lyrics of every song. The CD and book arrive tied with a ribbon.

Hanging Fishbowl

www.mxyplyzyk.com 🎁🎁

This fishbowl, designed to hang on a wall, makes standing in the corner more bearable.

Adopt an Animal

www.zoonewengland.com 🎁🎁/animal

Most local zoos offer a program where you can adopt an animal. At Zoo New England in Boston, you can choose from a number of large and exotic animals. The package includes an adoption certificate, color photograph of your chosen animal, an adorable plush animal, a Zoodoption sticker, fact sheet, and window decal. Your tax-deductible contribution will help the zoos' wildlife conservation efforts. Contact your local zoo and see if they have any adoption programs.

A Museum Art Class

www.mfah.com prices vary

Many museums have educational programs, some specifically designed to teach kids. In Houston, the Museum of Fine Arts has an entire school for education; it offers art classes for people of all ages. Select from classes in drawing, painting, sculpture, ceramics, printmaking, photography, jewelry making, book binding, computer art, cartooning, tile work, bookmaking, even furniture building.

Inflatable Submarine Ball Pit

www.7thavenuestore.com 🎁🎁

Doesn't every kid want one of these? An inflatable vinyl cage filled with hundreds of plastic balls is a fantasy realized. Set your scene; this one simulates a submarine.

Floating Trampoline

www.target.com 🎁🎁🎁🎁🎁

Instantly transform an ordinary lake into an amusement ride with a gigantic Aviva Orbit Inflatable Floating Trampoline. This enormous trampoline is designed to handle years of use and inflates easily with an electric pump.

"Fun with Your Dog" Science Kit

www.misterart.com 🎁

Keep them both busy with a kit from Scientific Explorer

that gives a kid a chance to know more than they ever imagined about their dog.

Bowling Ball

www.bowling.com 🎁🎁+

Spending time with the family is way more fun when you have your own Hello Kitty, Mickey Mouse, or Simpsons bowling ball.

S'mores Maker

www.wishingfish.com 🎁🎁

This city S'mores Maker Set comes with a central roaster, four roasting forks, and four ceramic trays, all on a rotating tray.

Tooth Fairy Pillows

www.trampolini.net 🎁

Makes losing your teeth a pleasant experience.

Share of Stock

www.oneshare.com 🎁🎁+

It's a nice gesture, even if they can't play with it. Choices include everything from Tiffany to Coca-Cola to GE to Chuck E. Cheese.

My Twinn Doll Gift Package

www.mytwinn.com 🎁🎁🎁

A little creepy, but definitely cool. The girl can create a doll in her own likeness: eight eye colors, four skin tones, and fifteen lifelike face molds created by master sculptors match a wide variety of children's face shapes. Also includes matching girl and doll charm bracelets.

Felt Donuts

www.sewdorky.com 🎁/each

Cute, but do not eat. Hand-stitched felt donuts including double chocolate, raspberry jelly filled, and Vermont maple—choice of a dozen flavors.

Professional Car Designer Kit

www.epartyunlimited.com 🎁

Everything a kid needs to design a cool ride. Kit comes with tracing underlays, color pencil set, blue line pencil, black marker, #2 pencil, template, paper stickers, and the car's complete step-by-step instruction book.

Oopsy Daisy Growth Chart

www.babyoliverboutique.com 🎁🎁

Adorable personalized growth chart keeps track of their height and doubles as wall art.

Kiddie Hummer

www.littletikes.com 🎁🎁🎁🎁

For tough kids only . . . a badass mini Hummer. The H2 by Little Tikes is powered by a rechargeable twelve-volt battery and features a five-song playlist, pretend GPS receiver, pretend seat belts, adjustable seats, aircraft-style gearshift, chrome-style grill, HUMMER wheels, rugged twelve-inch tires, tilt hood, hood latches, and large capacity storage. Will make you want one, too.

Fairy Wings Kit

www.niftycool.com 🎁

The Fairy Wings Kit comes with wings, puffy stickers,

glitter glue, organdy ribbons, daisy appliqués, one magic wand, and full instructions.

Kid's Forensic Lab

www.shopping.discovery.com 🎁🎁🎁

They may not stay up for *CSI*, but they'll enjoy this. The Discovery Whodunit? Forensics Lab comes with six cases and lab instruments to analyze handwriting, decipher blood type, and examine mysterious fibers.

Lil Driver Golf Cart

www.fantasytoyland.com 🎁🎁🎁🎁

The country club's calling. Kid's cart includes a horn, colorful novelty golf bag with three toy clubs plus balls and tees.

Playhouse Puppet Theater

www.alextoys.com 🎁🎁🎁🎁

Guaranteed hours of entertainment will be had in the My Playhouse sturdy wood and laminated panel puppet theater playhouse. It features a colorful frame and fabric curtains, a chalkboard, and a play clock.

Treeless Tree House

www.danielswoodland.com 🎁🎁🎁🎁🎁

Daniels Wood Land Tree Houses are self-standing tree houses that need no tree. Kids enter through the hollowed-out stump and climb a ladder into the upstairs playroom.

Life-Sized Playhouses

www.craftsburykids.com 🎁🎁🎁🎁+

Kids will go crazy for a gingerbread cottage, sheriff's house, or even a circus big top—just large enough for your kid and some pals.

Cute Kids' Umbrella

www.creationsbykim.com 🎁

Adults tend to go for the more generic black umbrella, but kids should be able to have more fun in the rain. Get them a special umbrella that looks like a frog, elephant, duck, even a ladybug.

Picture People Portrait Club

www.picturepeople.com 🎁🎁

The Picture People have over three hundred locations in the United States and offer great portrait packages. The Portrait Club offers free portrait sittings for a year, plus three free color portrait sheets up to an 8 × 10 sized sheet, one year storage of portrait negatives, plus other exclusive offers.

Leather Animal Bookends

www.cocoacrayon.com 🎁🎁🎁+

Leather Zoo's sweet 100 percent leather animals come in pairs to keep books neatly stored. Choose from elephants, dinosaurs, bunnies, giraffes, pigs, dragons, dogs, moose, lions, and a bull and bear combo.

Personalized Fleece Blanket

www.babybox.com 🎁🎁🎁

This colorful 29" × 40" fleece blanket has fleece appliqués and can be personalized with the kid's name.

Playful Wall Art

www.wallcandyarts.com 🎁🎁+

Peel and stick fun images to create a unique space for a kid. Bunnies, cows, and lambs are all part of their world. If you change your mind, you can unpeel and restick. Some kits come as a long border and others come in pieces.

The Little Prince Bookends

www.karikter.com 🎁🎁

Adorable for a child's room, these colorful wooden bookends celebrate the storybook character of *The Little Prince/Le Petit Prince.*

Kid's Art Turned Masterpiece

www.creationsbyyou.com 🎁

Good for the mini ego, My Masterpiece Kit comes with everything you need to turn your kid's drawing into an official museum masterpiece! The child's drawing is submitted and comes back as either a framed work of art on mock canvas (real canvas is a little extra) with a brass identification plate *or* you can elect to have the piece turned into an official museum poster print.

Kid Pouf

www.minijake.com 🎁🎁🎁

The Zid Zid Kid's soft cotton flannel, hand-drawn embroidered seat is fun for a kid to plop down on. Comes in a variety of styles.

Bilingual Doll

www.languagelittles.com

The Language Little International Dolls bring a foreign language into a kid's world. Each 16" doll speaks up to thirty different phrases and words in both English and a foreign language, including Spanish, French, Italian, Chinese, Japanese, Hebrew, Russian, Korean, German, and Greek.

Soft Story Toys

www.toyandbookstore.com

Pockets of Learning toys are an award-winning series for kids. Their Read and Play sets tell the tales of favorite classic stories. Each comes with a soft play set and corresponding fabric book. Choose from *Goldilocks*, *Little Red Riding Hood*, and *The Three Little Pigs.*

Tooth Fairy Box

www.goodnessforchildren.com

Put lost teeth in these little boxes and wait for the tooth fairy to come claim her prize. The box is 2.25" × 2.25", decorated with an enchanting image, and features an interior mirror and tiny pillow for a tooth.

Musical Skirt

www.babyscholars.com

A skirt that plays music? Operating with a motion sensor, this skirt plays *The Nutcracker Suite* while she dances around.

Alphabet Circle Rug

www.abcschoolsupply.com

This large oval rug is nearly 7' × 10' and is brightly designed with the letters of the alphabet.

Mask-Making Kit

www.abcschoolsupply.com

Kit comes with twenty-four precut masks made of card stock, along with stuff to decorate them, including colorful strings, buttons, beads, and stickers.

Barbar Rocker

www.karikter.com

How many kids get to ride an elephant in their own room? This wooden Barbar the Elephant rocker is made by the French toy company Vilac.

Scrabble Jr.

www.gamedaze.com

Get them working on their words at an early age.

Potato Sacks

www.abcschoolsupply.com

Set of six sturdy polyester potato sacks with nylon straps turns a potato sack race into the real deal. Each sack is a different color and has a number in four languages.

Ladybug Rolling Suitcase

www.samsonitecompanystores.com

This rolling luggage is in the shape of a ladybug. Made of durable polyester, it's 18" high and weighs under four pounds (empty).

Sturdy Kids' Step Stool

www.abigails.com 🎁🎁

These wooden step-up stools by M&M Designs come in several themes for boys and girls and can be personalized with the child's name for an extra $15.

The Original Peter Rabbit Books One to Twenty-three Presentation Box

http://us.penguingroup.com/ 🎁🎁🎁🎁

All twenty-three little books from Beatrix Potter's World of Peter Rabbit series are held in a decorated presentation box celebrating their one-hundredth anniversary. Each book's illustrations are delicately improved and reproduced.

Fun Hooks for Kids

www.karmakiss.com 🎁

Not every kid can say they hang their coat up on a dinosaur head. These silly hooks come in an assortment of creature heads: T-Rex, Para Dino, and Toro Dino.

BLIK Farm Wall Decals

www.notneutral.com 🎁🎁

These colorful wall decals will brighten up a kid's room easily. The BLIK Farm Wall Decals come in four sheets of decals in kiwi green, tomato red, yellow, and sky blue. Each sheet is 14" × 14" and made of self-adhesive, removable vinyl. Can also be applied to glass and wood.

Whimsy Animal Wall Clocks

www.karmakiss.com 🎁

These colorful kids' wall clocks make telling time fun. Choose from pig, cat, cow, monkey, frog, or bear.

The Harry Potter Time-Turner

www.noblecollection.com 🎁🎁

The Noble Collection offers an authentic re-creation of Hermione's Time-Turner featured in the movie *Harry Potter and the Prisoner of Azkaban*. The Time-Turner is centered with a working miniature hourglass, and its inner rings rotate. Plated in twenty-four karat gold, it's nearly two inches in diameter and hangs from an eighteen-inch chain. It also comes complete with a display.

Baby Cie Kids' Tea Party Set

www.polkadotwhale.com 🎁🎁

Baby Cie's Tea Set comes with four teacups, four biscuit plates, a sugar bowl, a creamer, and a teapot. All pieces are made of porcelain, and each has a different image on it: ballerina, butterfly, tiara, poodle, princess, and a honeybee.

Little Cook's Kit

www.sassafrasenterprises.com 🎁

Your kid will cook like a pro when using this kit's chef's hat, apron, oven mitts, and wooden spoon.

THE METROSEXUAL

Let's be perfectly clear . . . they are not gay. They may find delight in applying Kiehl's hair styling products, appreciate the difference between Barneys and Bendel's, even carry their Gucci man-purses with pride, but by definition, they are just well-groomed, nicely styled *heterosexual* men. Fortunately, the Metrosexual's affinity for life's aesthetics actually makes it easy to shop for him. Just ask yourself these simple questions: Will it enhance his dashing appearance? It's a winner. Does it flaunt his exquisite sense of style? No question it's perfect. Can it distinguish him from his gender mates sporting beer bellies and bad rugs? Even better. As long as his teeth twinkle and his designer duds dazzle, the Metrosexual will be grateful. And if you're lucky, maybe one day all of his primping and preening will rub off on the rest of the guys who think Hermès is a sexually transmitted disease.

Checklist Mirror
www.knockknock.biz
He'll never leave home with an imperfection.

Shape-Enhancing Underwear

www.internationalmale.com 🎁

Boxer briefs come with a padded front pouch for those who need a little help.

Hair Gel to Go

www.aveda.com 🎁

Aveda's Control Tape Extreme Style Strips will fix any do in a jiffy. Just wet your hands and the strip dissolves into instant gel for application.

Hermès Silk Tie

www.hermes.com 🎁🎁🎁

Classic Hermès *H* silk twill tie is a sharp accent piece.

Head Razor

www.headblade.com 🎁

The revolutionary razor made for a scalp shave so easy you can do it using just one finger.

Urban Man Bag

www.manhattanportage.com 🎁🎁

It's only 7.5" × 9" × 2.5" and is perfect for an iPod, a cell phone, wallet, keys, etc. Manhattan Portage's Urban Bag is city chic and made of virtually indestructible Cordura Plus nylon, has loads of pockets, and comes in six different colors.

Luxurious Boxers

www.threadcountzzz.com 🎁🎁/pair

Ultrahigh thread count boxers come in matching drawstring pouch; 100 percent Egyptian cotton fabric.

Manicure Set

www.groominglounge.com

The Dovo Deluxe Manicure Set will keep his hands neat and tidy. The leather case is filled with cuticle/nail scissors, fingernail clippers, a diamond nail file, tweezers, and a cuticle pusher tool.

Shaving Set by L'Occitane

www.loccitane.com 

The L'Occitan shaving set comes with lightly scented shaving gel and aftershave balm.

Teeth Whitening Kit

www.americarx.com

A smile makes a first impression—and you know these guys want theirs to shine. The Rembrandt Plus Superior Bleaching System comes with everything they'll need to help get their pearly whites whiter.

Detox Skin Care Kit

www.biotherm-usa.com

Help him fight the damaging effects of pollution with the Hydra-Det0$_2$X Starter Kit: Detoxifying Cleanser, Detoxifying Moisturizer, Detoxifying Eye Gel, and mask.

Botox Session

www.botoxcosmetic.com prices vary

Stressed but don't want to look it? Old but don't want to look that either? Get Botox. Site will direct you to a licensed physician who administers Botox.

Hair Removal

www.mesotherapy411.com prices vary

Mesotherapy is a medical treatment that involves injecting small amounts of natural plant extracts, homeopathic agents, pharmaceutical agents, and vitamins into the skin to treat a variety of conditions, including hair removal. Go to the site to find a physician in your area.

Classic Robe Gift

www.startreatment.com 🎁🎁🎁

He can lounge in style in Star Treatment's Classic Gift of a handsome micro-chenille oatmeal robe and Sante Provence spa line of shampoo, soap, and candles.

Burberry Plaid Boxers

www.saks.com 🎁🎁

Burberry's signature check pattern comes on cotton boxers.

Tanning Bed

www.bbqguys.com 🎁🎁🎁🎁🎁

A healthy glow makes everyone look better. Owning your own tanning bed makes it easy to get one. Seventy-six-inch Pearl 16 bed features sixteen Phillips performance lamps and comes complete with a head pad and goggles.

Fancy Pants PJs

www.brooksbrothers.com 🎁🎁+

Sleep in style with monogrammed 100 percent cotton pajamas in a selection of fabrics and styles.

Starter Grooming Kit

www.anthony.com

🎁🎁

The Essentials Starter Kit grooming kit for budding metrosexuals takes the mystery out of personal care.

Paint-by-Numbers Photo

www.futurememories.com

🎁🎁🎁

It's a self-portrait made easy—and with this, he'll spend hours working on his own face. Send in a photo, and you'll get a printed canvas and charted graph of the pic. The kit includes paints, brushes, chipboard, and instructions.

Manly Shave Set

www.crabtree-evelyn.com

🎁🎁🎁

The Edwin Jagger three-piece Shave Set comes with a badger shave brush, razor, and a standing holder. It's made of brass and faux ivory.

Brooks Brothers Cashmere-Blend Sock

www.brooksbrothers.com

🎁🎁

Luxurious warmth for your feet in a cashmere-and-nylon-blend sock that comes in a dozen handsome colors. Hand wash only.

Bally Sauna Suit

www.taylorgifts.com

🎁

He can wear this silver suit while exercising or even while just puttering around—and lose extra inches by doing it. The Bally vinyl sauna suit helps you shed water weight by keeping body heat sealed in to help muscles stay warm.

Gentleman's Guide to Style and Grooming

www.barnesandnoble.com

Barnes and Noble published this essential book for the metrosexual. Need to know how to tie a tie? Where to go for a professional shave? Want to know why shoes are so important? All of these answers and more are provided in this must-have metro bible.

China Martini Glass Cufflinks

www.detailsart.com

Designed by Sonia Spencer of the U.K., these hand decorated square cufflinks are made of bone china, and each has a handsome martini glass on it.

Crocodile Cufflink Box

www.vivre.com

Where do guys put their accessories? In a convenient crocodile carrying case! These glazed croc boxes are lined in leather and come in an assortment of colors.

Leather Money Clip

www.redenvelope.com

The Belden leather money clip is a masculine and stylish way for him to keep his cash. It can be monogrammed for an additional fee. Available in blue, chocolate, rust, and black.

Fogless Lighted Shower Mirror

www.brookstone.com

He can shave in the shower safely with this dual LED-lit mirror. It mounts to nearly any smooth surface and has two razor holders.

Men's Deluxe Eyebrow Grooming Kit

www.eyebrowz.com 🎁🎁

Say good-bye to the unibrow with this kit to clean up his brow. Inside a plastic pouch are three brow razors, brow scissors and trimming brush, white outliner stick, a comb/brush, six stencils, and instructions.

Tan Towel

www.magellans.com 🎁

The easiest tan to get yet. Wipe on one of these disposable towelettes, and your fake bake lasts for a week. It won't streak, stain, or wash off. Ten towelettes per order.

THE GIFTED GOURMET

Who knew that a small cheese from Verona is called a *caciotta*? The Gifted Gourmet does. They're the friends you proudly put in charge of ordering wine at a restaurant. When they throw a dinner party, you're prepared for a five-course tasting menu, complete with sorbet intermezzo to cleanse the palette. They shop at epicurean markets, not grocery stores; eat game, not meat; use china, not Chinette. The Gifted Gourmets may seem to have it all, but there are always things even experts don't get themselves, and that's where you can fill in the blanks. Instead of counting on them to order a fine wine, how about tempting them to make it themselves with a do-it-yourself kit? Or treat them to a regional delicacy with some assistance from the United States Postal Service. And then there's always the latest and greatest in culinary gear from designer dishware to ambitious accessories. Don't feel intimidated shopping for them, even if you're not a kitchen connoisseur. Besides, you might luck out and get to spend an intimate evening enjoying your gift firsthand.

Meringues for the Memories

www.justmeringues.com 🎁🎁/100 cookies

Order up some of these unique, one-of-a-kind confections that can be table decoration as well as dessert! These flavorful and colorful meringues are special sweet treats that feature a personalized message sticking out of each airy piece. Choose from a variety of flavors, fillings, colors, and toppings. Some unique options include cinnamon, toffee crunch, and pumpkin spice.

Cookie Cutter Crafting Kit

www.foosecookiecutters.com 🎁

Gives new meaning to making cookies from scratch—start by designing custom cookie cutters. This all-in-one kit comes with 72" of bendable solid copper strip, 16" of permanent easy-to-use dry film adhesive, working base and forming tools for convenient accurate forming, starter patterns, and recipes.

Crab Cakes on Demand

www.crabcakeexpress.com 🎁🎁/8 cakes

These Maryland crab cakes are 100 percent lump blue crabmeat—no bread or other fillings. Lumpy and delicious, they can be frozen or used in another recipe.

Essential Oils for Cooking

www.rafalspicecompany.com 🎁+

Want to get the essence of a flavor in your cooking without adding the actual ingredient? Switch to a cooking oil made from that item. There are hundreds to choose from including Anise, Pumpkin, Cedar Leaf, and Siberian Fir Needle.

NapaStyle Spice Box

www.napastyle.com 🎁🎁🎁

This elegant acacia wood box comes filled with ten different NapaStyle salts and spices.

Digital Wine Cooler

www.smarthome.com 🎁🎁🎁🎁

They'll never have to worry about storing bottles at the right temperature. This countertop digital wine cooler holds six bottles and maintains a perfect temperature for wine storage.

Gorgeous Chocolates

www.jinpatisserie.com 🎁🎁

Twenty pieces of uniquely flavored chocolates come packaged beautifully in a silk box. Some of the exotic flavors include Sea Salt Caramel, Lemon Grass, Jasmine, Black Roasted Sesame, Lychee, and more.

Kitchen of Provence

www.penzeys.com 🎁🎁🎁

They'll be set with a Pensey's Spices gift crate of classic spices for seasoning French foods, including bouquet garni, fennel seed, sweet paprika, vanilla beans, and French lavender.

Invent Your Own Ice Cream

www.ecreamery.com 🎁🎁🎁/4 quarts (minimum)

Create your own ice cream. Pick your flavor from over sixty choices (like cucumber, rose, pumpkin pie, lavender, or plain old cream), with over sixty toppings (like thyme, basil, mint leaves, pop rocks candies, cheddar cheese bits, coffee-soaked ladyfingers) and a base mix (gelato, classic ice cream, or super premium ice cream, which is richer).

Authentic Lobster Boil

www.livelob.com 🎁🎁🎁/two one-pound live lobsters

The Lobster Gram Deluxe will send live lobsters to anywhere in the United States, along with the cooking pot and other lobster accessories.

Foie Gras Set

www.henryandlulu.com 🎁🎁🎁

Classic Laguiole design by Claude Dozorme will come in handy at their next gourmet dinner party.

Cheesecake Club

http://shop.thecheesecakefactory.com 🎁/month (7" cake)

The Cheesecake Factory's Cheesecakes by the Month club will send one of their famous cheesecakes out every month for a year.

Wine Cozy

www.builtny.com 🎁

Perfect for a picnic, supersleek soft-sided two-bottle wine carrier comes in an assortment of festive colors.

Deluscious Cookies

www.delusciouscookies.com 🎁🎁/dozen; milk is an extra $5

A pizza box filled with one-of-a-kind cookie flavors, along with a jug of milk. Flavors include rocky road, wild blueberry lemon and white chocolate, and chocolate bing cherry.

Caviar and Delicacies

www.caviar.com 🎁+

Seattle Caviar Company sells quality caviar, truffles, foie gras, and even lessons so a wannabe can sound like they know what they're talking about.

Vintage Posters

www.postergroup.com 🎁🎁🎁🎁+

Original vintage posters advertising liquors and various gourmet foods will inspire any gourmet.

Old-Fashioned Candy

www.hometownfavorites.com 🎁+

For the candy connoisseur, find everything from Sen-Sen to Teaberry gum to Zotz. Gift collections are available.

Wine Master Pocket Guide

www.jr.com 🎁

The Excalibur electronic pocket guide provides instant access to more than 10,000 wine ratings and reviews. It includes a wine glossary and tasting terms, wine basics for beginners, best buys, editor's picks, and cellar buys.

Wine-Making Kit

www.cabelas.com 🎁🎁

Encourage them to channel Lucy and Ethel and make their own wine. Kit includes the gear they need to get started: fermenter/bottling bucket combo, glass carboy, racking/siphoning equipment, Portuguese double lever corker, eight packs of C-Brite sanitizer, and a pack of thirty Altec corks. Will make thirty bottles.

Deep Dish Chicago Pizza

www.Ginoseast.com +

Give an original Chicago-style deep dish pizza from Chicago's most famous pizza parlor, Gino's East. Choose from sausage, spinach, pepperoni, or cheese. Arrives frozen.

Drunken Figs

www.cocoavino.com /box of four

These deluxe organic figs are soaked in port and then dipped into creamy chocolate. Figs arrive gift packaged in a tin with satin ribbon.

Build-Your-Own Coffee

www.jlhufford.com /one-pound bag

JL Hufford Coffee and Tea sells coffees only from the top 3 percent of the highest quality of coffee from the Arabica family. If you want to invent your own flavor, their Build-Your-Own Blended Coffee feature will allow you to select up to eight exotic flavors and create your own blend. Flavor choices include toffee, cinnamon, hazelnut, orange, and many more.

Culinary Vacation Adventures

www.gapadventures.com

G.A.P. Adventures specializes in vacation packages that honor the people and land where you travel. Their grassroots approach takes you off the beaten path and into an authentic experience. They offer several culinary adventures—gourmet trips that go into the markets of local villages and include cooking classes to learn local techniques. You can select trips that take you to Japan, Vietnam, Argentina, Italy, France, and India, to name just a few.

Larousse Gastronomique Culinary Encyclopedia

www.amazon.com

First published in 1938, the 1,360-page *Larousse Gastronomique* is the culinary encyclopedia for the serious chef. It tends to focus on the classic continental culinary tradition but has expanded to include some American cooking. Larousse is the go-to reference guide for information on culinary terms and also includes more than 3,500 recipes and gorgeous color photographs.

Professional Chef's Hat

www.complimentstothechef.com

Adult chef hat has a Velcro adjustment and comes in classic white or red.

Specialty Food Club Membership

www.stonewallkitchen.com /six-month membership

Stonewall Kitchen offers a Specialty Food Club membership, where a lucky recipient gets a new basket of Stonewall Kitchen gourmet delicacies each month. One month may be the Farmhouse Pancake and Waffle Mix with Maine maple syrup, wild blueberry jam, and raspberry peach champagne jam. Another month could be a gourmet cracker and tapenade set that includes Asiago cheese, Down East crackers, and artichoke and caper relish; or it could be a triple fudge brownie mix with a jar of black cherry cognac sauce.

Chef's Cucina Hand Care Duo

www.ebubbles.com

A chef's hands will take a beating. This Cucina combo of hand wash and lotion is delicate enough for hands that are washed frequently. Sets come in Coriander and Olive Tree or Ginger and Sicilian Lemon.

Gourmet Chocolate Tablettes

www.debauveandgallais.com

Order up a set of ten exotic chocolate bars. Mix and match your preferred flavors, and they come wrapped with Debauve & Gallais's trademark insignia.

Gourmet Olive Oil Bottles

www.sbceramicstore.com 

For anyone who makes their own oils, these hand-painted bottles will make their creations even more special. Forty-eight styles available.

THE CAMPUS UNDERGRAD

Ah, you remember college—the days of beer and roses. An institution of "higher" learning. Let's be honest: the biggest lesson you learned in college wasn't in a classroom but at registration when you became known as a number, not a name. Suddenly the world seemed colossal, and you accepted the fact that you are merely a speck. There are ways we can help college students feel human again; in fact, they're pretty easy to please. Living in a fifteen-square-foot dorm room, they're always looking for ways to make the box feel more personal: a flower here, a photo there, a token of their school spirit anywhere. They also want to impress their friends (and avoid studying) with the latest gear, so any sort of gadget/electronic/toy is a guaranteed hit. Of course, there's the quickest way to their hearts: *food!* (A) it's a free meal, and (B) it reminds them of home, which—believe it or not—they miss. Don't hold back; make sure to let them know you miss them, too—provided, of course, it doesn't interrupt their Saturday night.

Initial Towel Set

www.ink-well.net

College gals can bathe in style with a soft terry towel sporting a single monogrammed initial. Set comes with one bath and one hand towel.

Adagio Tea Starter Set

www.adagio.com

The ingenuiTEA Starter Gift Set comes with an innovative tea maker that brews fresh teas quickly. Drop loose tea leaves into container, fill with hot water, let it steep, then put it on top of a mug, and a valve opens to let the tea out underneath. Mesh filter keeps leaves from getting into the tea. Set includes four tins of sample teas.

Tabletop Beer Tap

www.tabletappers.com

The bong-like beer tap means you don't have to get up from the table to get another beer. Holds 116 ounces of ice-cold beer.

College Sneaker Slippers

www.onlyslippers.com

These stuffed slippers look like big sneakers and come in school colors with the team logo.

Ring Bottle Opener

www.thinkgeek.com

Beer drinking has just gotten easier. The Original Ring Thing stainless steel ring looks cool and doubles as a bottle opener—you don't even have to take it off your hand for it to work.

MTV Video Music Awards Collection

www.amazon.com 🎁/each

DVDs that feature all the rock or all of the hip pop musical performances from past Video Music Awards shows. Also includes host monologues.

Bottle Opener Sandals

www.active-sandals.com 🎁🎁

Who knew life could be this convenient? A bottle opener built into the sole of the Reef Fanning flip-flops makes a day at the beach a whole lot easier.

Collegiate Toss Pillow

www.collegiategifts.com 🎁

Every college student will want to show off their school spirit and decorate with a bright toss pillow. Go team!

Gardens in a Bag

www.pottingshedcreations.com 🎁

Grow everything from flowers to herbs to vegetables on a windowsill out of this adorable bag.

College Lithographs

www.brownson5th.com 🎁🎁🎁

These lithographs of most college landmarks come color print laminated in 3-D on a reverse shadow box. Choice of black, burgundy, or green matte, 18" × 14".

Swarovski Crystal Sorority Sets

www.inyourskivvies.com 🎁🎁

Bling out a tank and boy shorts with sorority letters.

Simplified Coffeemaker

www.1to1coffee.com 🎁🎁

The easiest coffeemaker around. Just drop the teabag-ish pod of coffee into the machine for a perfect single dose in under a minute.

Customized Hoodie

www.neighborhoodies.com 🎁🎁

Design a classic zip-up hoodie and represent whatever you think needs representing.

Student Discount Card

www.studentadvantage.com 🎁/year

Students can save money on travel, school gear, entertainment, food, and more.

Caffeinated Soap

www.thinkgeek.com 🎁/one bar

Wake up with a jolt when using the Shower Shock Caffeinated Soap; it has 200 milligrams of caffeine per washing.

Badass TV Tray

www.mcphee.com 🎁🎁

Wild flames greet them when they plant themselves in front of the tube and feed their faces.

Minibike to Go

www.extremescooters.biz 🎁🎁🎁🎁

It's a bike . . . it's a scooter . . . it's the Pukka GX400C Electric Minibike, and this miniature ride looks cool anywhere on campus.

Flowers in a Can

www.uncommongoods.com 🎁

No garden? Here are flowers made easy. In a set of two flowers, each kit comes in an elegant and colorful tin can. Immediately brightens up a dorm room.

Arcade Games

www.arcadegames.com 🎁🎁🎁🎁🎁

Pac-Man . . . Asteroids . . . Space Invaders . . . They're all here brand-new.

Get-Yo-Ass-Up Clock

www.appliancehut.com 🎁🎁

The Sonic Alert Sonic Boom Vibrating Alarm Clock does the job instead of their mothers.

Hangover Mask

www.beauty.com 🎁

For those weekend mornings, the Oscar + Dehn Hangover from Hell Cooling Eye Mask was designed with drinkers in mind.

Cleaning Service

www.mollymaid.com 🎁🎁🎁

Help them help themselves by providing a housecleaning service. Molly Maid has offices in most major cities.

School Spirit

www.replicastadiums.com 🎁🎁+

Rah-rah! Mini replicas of college sports stadiums come in a variety of styles. The tiny fans are even sporting school colors.

A Morning Nosh

www.bagelboss.com 🎁🎁

Such a mitzvah! The New York Breakfast Gift Box 1 delivers bagels, lox, and cream cheese fresh.

Home-Cooked Dinner

www.alazing.com 🎁+

Meat loaf and potatoes . . . turkey and stuffing . . . Mom-complete meals, just like home.

The Write Stuff

www.fabulousstationery.com 🎁🎁

Quirky customized stationery for when an e-mail won't cut it. Stationery can be personalized with their name and a clever illustration.

Party Paraphernalia

www.aspecialgift.com 🎁🎁

A sleek leather Collabri combo flask and cigarette holder is perfect for the professional partier.

Beer Every Month

www.greatclubs.com 🎁🎁/month

Got beer? Take a break for the gourmet flavor of the month from the Great American Beer Club.

Serve It Up

www.plumparty.com 🎁

Baseball mitt–shaped chip 'n' dip bowl is appropriate for the macho entertainer.

Down-Home Barbecue

www.saltlickbbq.com 🎁🎁+

Authentic BBQ from Texas Hill Country's favorite spot. Order up smoked brisket, sausage, ribs, turkey, chicken, potato salad, and beans. Top it off with some pecan pie.

Casino Night

www.chipsandgames.com 🎁🎁

Instant Poker/Blackjack Table Top—just put over existing card table for a gambling good time. Each place has a plastic tray built in to hold onto a drink and poker chips. Poker game on one side and blackjack on the other.

Mounted Faux Animal Head

www.animalhead.com 🎁🎁🎁+

Every kind of animal head is available, including a T. rex and other dinosaur pals. No real animals or fur is used.

Hot Diggity Dogger Hot Dog Cooker/Toaster

www.hammacher.com 🎁🎁

This cool gadget conveniently cooks two hot dogs and toasts two buns simultaneously to make cooking hot dogs even easier than it already was.

University Bedding

www.universalshopping.com 🎁🎁

Sleep in spirit with a Tailgate Town collegiate sheet set. Available in full or queen, each set comes with a top sheet and two pillowcases, all stamped with the school's logo.

Collegiate Tailgate Canopy

www.universalshopping.com

Tailgate Town's University Tailgate Canopy features the school's colors and logo on all four sides. The 9' × 9' frame holds up a water-resistant canopy that's about 6' high.

Over-the-Door Shoe Organizer

www.garnethill.com

Dorm rooms are too small—and that's before they show up with their shoe collection. The Garnet Hill shoe caddy has twenty pockets, keeps shoes organized and out of the way, and adds some color to the room.

Alma Mater Slippers

www.hammacher.com

These indoor/outdoor suede clog-like slippers have a fuzzy fleece inside and the school insignia on the top. Fifty universities available.

The Kegerator

www.beveragefactory.com

The Danby Beer Keg Cooler is able to convert from keg cooler to straight-up refrigerator. It has a stainless steel door, a 5.8-cubic-foot capacity, and all the parts needed to pour a cold beer.

School Spirit Mailbox Wrap

www.curbdecor.com

They can show their school spirit by wrapping their mailbox with their favorite college team logo. Mail Wraps are made of sturdy vinyl and attach to the mailbox with magnets on each side of the cover.

Collegiate Golf Balls

www.enjoylifeinc.com 🎁

Golf balls emblazoned with the logos from dozens of colleges and universities across the United States.

Barbara K Dorm Survival Tool Kit

www.homedepot.com 🎁

This practical kit contains everything you need to hang pictures, posters, and curtains. Dorm Survival Tool Kit comes with a hammer, scissors, screwdriver, tape measure, flashlight, and more, all held in a snazzy backpack.

Monopoly: College Style

www.lateforthesky.com 🎁

Just like a regular Monopoly game, but customized to a particular university. Board features popular landmarks on that school's campus, and tokens are symbols appropriate to the school. Forty-five school options.

Domino's Gift Certificate

www.dominos.com $15 minimum

Bet you didn't know Domino's Pizza sells gift certificates. They're available in increments of $5.

Neon Pub Clock

www.beveragefactory.com 🎁🎁🎁+

Put one of these over the bar, and your home will be the new pub in town. Neon clocks feature designs from Harley-Davidson and Jack Daniel's.

Laundry Bag

www.packhappy.com 🎁🎁

This oversized laundry bag made of nylon oxford cloth has an embroidered design and the words "The Great Unwashed."

THE PRINCESS

Some may say she's high-maintenance, demanding, and expensive. But you think she's the belle of the ball. Always perfectly put together, she's dazzling in diamonds and stunning in stilettos. She's your personal reference guide for up-and-coming designers, hot places to shop, even new trends in food. With her, you have a dedicated style council; that's why for the Princess, no ordinary gift will do. You know she has refined taste, so one-of-a-kind beauty products and amenities created especially for her will complement her tacit tiara. Simple items upgraded with silk, suede, or sequins will surely make her majesty swoon. And since every day should feel like a spa day, ritzy and glitzy activities that maintain her overall magnificence will guarantee you a special place in her court. The Princess prefers the finer things in life, so treat her like the royalty she aspires to be.

Princess Mug

www.abernook.com

Sixteen-ounce mug with "Princess" branded across it.

Deluxe Ultrasonic Jewelry Cleaner and Tarnish Remover

www.sharperimage.com 🎁🎁🎁

Just fill with water, and ultrasonic waves will miraculously clean jewelry in five minutes in places a brush won't reach. Swap the water for silver tarnish remover and you've got it covered.

Ultra-Absorbent Personalized Towels

www.llbean.com 🎁/+$5 monogramming

Superthick and soft, these heavy-duty towels can be monogrammed for a special treat.

Swarovski Crystal Domino Set

www.neimanmarcus.com 🎁🎁🎁🎁

A real gem of a game. An exclusive Neiman Marcus domino set studded with Swarovski crystal numbers. Comes in a pink leather case.

Frownies Face-Lift in a Bag

www.frownies.com 🎁🎁🎁

Not sold on the plastic surgery route? Frownies are a good sub. They're facial pads that claim to retrain your facial muscles to relax and leave a younger, wrinkle-free surface. Recommended use is for the forehead and corners of the eyes and mouth. Set comes with Frownies Pads plus biologically active skin care treatments.

At-Home Airbrush Tanner

www.alltvstuff.com 🎁

Think of it as body art. Spray on a tan with an easy-to-use airbrush; comes with three tanning cartridges.

Stylish Shoe Bags

www.keptcouture.com 🎁

Keep shoes scuff-free and clothes clean by using practical shoe bags when traveling. Plus they're cute.

Personalized Ring

www.artcarved.com 🎁🎁🎁🎁 (genuine stone, 14k band)

From the Stackable collection, select an Irresistible ring to stack with others. Engrave it with a special date or name and choose her favorite stone. Choose between a genuine or fake stone and white or yellow gold.

Head-to-Toe Body Kit

www.latherup.com 🎁

Lather's exclusive products come in a useful four-piece one-ounce-sized Head-to-Toe Pampering Kit: AHA Hand Creme, Bamboo Lemongrass Foaming Body Scrub, Manuka Body Butter, and Lavender and Eucalyptus Foot Creme. It doesn't miss a part.

AntiAging Kit

www.drugstore.com 🎁

L'Oreal's ReNoviste Glycolic Peel Kit aims to restructure skin by simulating cell turnover and enhancing production of collagen and elastin. Visibly reduces lines and firms wrinkled skin.

Leather Yoga Bag

www.startreatment.com 🎁🎁🎁🎁

This Urban Yoga Tote leather bag has been specifically designed to handle a diva's yoga mat. There is also a special compartment for cell phone and keys and extra room for yoga accessories.

Pocket Mirror

www.henryandlulu.com 🎁🎁

Patina's pocket mirror in a colorful leather case—opens to a regular and a magnifying mirror. Leather comes in lime, almond, orange, sky blue, or red.

Stylish Sleep Mask

www.crisnotti.com 🎁

Choose from over sixty-two fabulously wonderful patterns with these sleep masks.

Aluminum Take-Out Container

www.propertopper.com 🎁🎁

No more paper cartons! Aluminum take-out container is designed to perfectly hold a Chinese take-out carton. Comes with chopsticks.

Discontinued Fragrances

www.thefragrancefactory.com prices vary

Good for someone whose favorite scent has faded away into history.

Perfumed Sensual Ice Cubes

www.kenzousa.com 🎁🎁

These perfumed Kenzoki Rice Steam Ice Cubes are made of plant water extracted from the rice plant. The ice cubes melt into a luscious and scented liquid that moisturizes the skin.

Anti-Cellulite Sneakers

www.blissworld.com 🎁🎁🎁🎁

Masai Barefoot Technology (MBT) anti-cellulite sneaker cushions your feet while providing your legs with a workout. Clinical studies suggest that regular use improves balance, posture, and circulation.

Luxury Slippers

www.amyjogladstone.com 🎁🎁🎁

Shear Bliss Leather Scuff with shearling lining are from the Spa Collection.

Swim in Style

www.homebodyheaven.com 🎁

Help her look cute and coordinated on the beach. Plastic mat comes packaged in a matching plastic tote bag.

Designer Purse Club

www.bagborroworsteal.com 🎁+

Get her several months of an online service where she can borrow the latest designer purse for a month. At the end of her session, she'll have the option to buy that bag with a significant discount.

Customized Flip-Flops

www.elizab.com 🎁🎁

Select a ribbon color and a printed motif to customize her favorite thongs.

Beauty Makeover Customer Service

www.maccosmetics.com prices vary

Get a free consultation at any M-A-C location (including

department store counters) with a trained makeup artist. Or, M-A-C store locations will offer private lessons for someone who needs to learn a little in the facial area. Afterwards, treat her to the expected purchases of the recommended products.

Satin and Mink Eye Mask

www.henryandlulu.com 🎁🎁🎁🎁

Gutzees mink sleep mask comes in a matching silk satin case and helps a princess find her slumber. In pink, brown, white, or natural.

Gucci Candle

www.gucci.com 🎁🎁🎁

A brown candle in a glass etched with the Gucci monogram has an exotic musky smell.

Sephora Freedom

www.sephora.com prices vary

Get her a gift card to Sephora, and you've made a Princess a very happy girl. This cosmetics boutique has one of the largest selections of bath and beauty products around. She can pick something from her favorite brands or try out a new designer.

Diamonds!

www.tiffany.com prices vary

You could find diamond earrings at your local jewelry store, but if you want to throw some icing on top of that bling, give them to her in that famous little blue Tiffany box.

Semipermanent Cosmetics

www.cosmeticpen.com

These Magic Stylo easy-to-apply cosmetics pens work with pigment that actually soaks into the skin, as opposed to being applied on top of it. The color lasts up to twenty-four hours and can be removed with ordinary makeup remover. The pens come in colors for lips, eyes, and eyebrows.

Get Fresh Hand Therapy Anti-Aging Hand Kit

www.beautyexclusive.com

Keep your hands looking young with Get Fresh's Hand Therapy. It includes a six-step process that protects and corrects the damage done. To protect, there's a hand cleanser, hand cream, and cuticle cream; to correct, there's a treatment, a serum, and a mask.

GoSMILE GoALL OUT Kit

www.beautyexclusive.com

This *GoSMILE* GoALL OUT tooth-whitening kit claims to whiten your teeth up to ten shades in just one week. With the set, you get fourteen ampoules of the Advanced Formula B1, seven ampoules of the daily whitening maintenance, midday brush and breath freshener in a silver compact, and a travel-sized duo a.m./p.m. whitening protection fluoride toothpaste.

Le Chic Chick Knowledge Cards

www.lechicchick.com

Each Le Chic Chick box comes with three decks of cards filled with answers to everything you need to know about being a chic chick. Decks are *The Elegance Deck* (how to be a proper lady), *The Strength Deck* (how to be a strong woman), and *The Intelligence Deck* (anything from "The Anatomy of an Orchestra" to "The Nine Noble Women" to "How to Say 'Hello' in Twenty-seven Languages").

Customized Crystal Champagne Flute

www.shoploveme.com

A chic crystal champagne flute with a person's initial on it in Swarovski crystals makes the bubbly much more special.

Pavé Faux Diamond Photo Frame

www.shoploveme.com /4 × 6 frame

Splurge on this sparkly diamondesque picture frame and draw everyone's attention to her favorite snapshot.

Monogrammed Shower Cap

www.spa1221.com

This black shower cap can be ordered with a customized monogram—as sleek as a cap can get.

Candletinis

www.gotgreatgifts.com

Don't try to drink this ten-ounce martini glass filled with a seventy-five-hour-burning candle. Candletini flavors come in apple, cosmo, chocolate, lemon, vanilla, and mango.

Oprah Bistro Mug

http://boutique.oprah.com

Giving someone an Oprah mug is like bringing them closer to the queen herself.

Uptown Girls Coasters

www.sbceramicstore.com

🎁

Set of six coasters represent all facets of a Princess's personality: they feature an image and title on each, like "Champagne Girl" and "Style Girl." Ceramic top with cork bottom; comes packaged in a gift box.

Fabric Tennis Racket Case

www.tossdesigns.com

🎁🎁

Toss Resort Gear has a distinct style of its own. The quilted tennis racket cover has an adjustable strap, comes in Toss's signature dot design, and is available in black, green, orange, or pink.

Assouline Memoire Slipcase

www.assoulineusa.com

🎁🎁🎁

Assouline has assembled a collection of classic memoirs of five fashion houses: Dior, Chloé, Roberto Cavalli, Dolce & Gabbana, and Emilio Pucci. Each hardcover book features glossy color and black-and-white images and walks you though the history of each house. The book set is housed in an elegant earth-toned fabric case.

The Luxe Robe

www.plushnecessities.com

🎁🎁🎁

You'd usually have to go to a spa to get this sort of glamour in a robe, but not anymore. The Luxe Robe has a soft terry inside and brushed microfiber on the outside. Available in five shades.

Princess Notes Panama Book

www.smython.com 🎁🎁

She can keep track of her favorite stores, cafés, and spas with this 5.5" × 3.5" pink leather, silver-edged paper notebook. The cover is stamped "Princess Notes" in silver.

Monogrammed Soaps

www.redenvelope.com 🎁🎁

The set of four triple-milled soaps comes in lavender, green tea, vanilla almond, freesia, or an assortment. Each soap can be monogrammed with initials or a name up to ten characters.

Kitson Ceramic Accessory Dish

www.shopkitson.com 🎁🎁

These hand-painted accessory dishes are made exclusively for Kitson. Three adorable styles each have three sections for earrings, bracelets, and rings.

THE RELIABLE 'RENTS

They gently patched booboos with kisses and Band-Aids and unconditionally supported you through college. On the other hand, they also got pee in their faces when changing your diapers and were forced to apologize to the neighbors when you killed their cat. Parents have seen it all and probably know you better than anyone else in the universe. So far, their reward for the years of toil and sacrifice is knowing you've turned out pretty well. But that doesn't cut it; they deserve more. They deserve a romantic weekend alone together where everything is free. They deserve a sentimental photograph customized in a unique and exclusive way. And they undoubtedly deserve to be spoiled with an indulgence that will make them feel like royalty and have their friends hinting to their own children. You owe them big for everything they've put up with over the years. And while they say your love and affection are enough of a gift, it's time to finally thank them properly for dealing with that dead cat.

Grilling Personalized Branding Iron

www.napastyle.com 🎁🎁🎁

Dad will take even more pride in his barbecue cooking when he brands his initials onto a steak. The stainless steel branding iron with wood handle comes packaged in a branded wooden box.

Bath-of-the-Month Club

www.smallflower.com 🎁🎁🎁+

Each month, treat mom to a relaxing and energizing luxury bath.

Personalized Pub Pitcher

www.catalogfavorites.com 🎁🎁/pitcher; 🎁🎁/four glasses

Kind of makes it clear who's the king of the party. A handsome pub beer pitcher and pint glasses are personalized with an inscribed name. Pitcher holds sixty ounces.

Custom Photo Pillow

www.exposuresonline.com 🎁🎁🎁

Send in a black-and-white or color photo, and it will be turned into a one-of-a-kind Ultrasuede throw pillow. Available in red, chocolate, or black.

Putting Challenge Ultimate Edition

www.arcadegames.com 🎁🎁🎁🎁🎁

The shape of this putting green physically changes electronically. It's programmed with four different eighteen-hole courses to practice putts on. A keyboard keeps your score.

Rearview Mirror and Camera

www.qualitymobilevideo.com

Calling all bad drivers: This back-up camera system is here to help. The small camera is built into a license plate frame and shoots what's immediately behind the car. The image is sent to a monitor that's mounted up front.

Poker Set

www.startreatment.com

The all-inclusive poker set provides a night of high-stakes entertainment. Comes with chips, cards, and dice in a sleek carrying case.

Yamuna Footsaver's Kit

www.yamunabodyrolling.com

Tell Mom to take a load off and treat her feet to pure pleasure. These plastic half spheres claim to improve alignment and muscle tone, stimulate reflexology points, strengthen arches, increase range of motion, and elongate the muscles of the calves, thighs, hips, and lower back. Comes with an instructional CD or DVD.

Photo Mobile

www.shopexit9.com

This special mobile shows off their favorite photos without taking up any shelf space.

Exotic Truffle Gift Box

www.vosgeschocolate.com

Exotic sixteen-piece truffle collection in the most unusual flavors including absinthe, ambrosia, and viola.

Leather Photo Bookmarks

www.henryandlulu.com

Patina's Moc Croc Calf or Leather Picture Frame Bookmarks come in a variety of bright colors and save a spot with a favorite photo.

Shoe Care Kit

www.johnstonmurphy.com

Dad will never be without a well-shined shoe. The Johnston & Murphy Shoe Care Kit comes with two shades of cream, two brush applicators, leather balm, two shine mitts, a shoehorn and brush, all housed in a cedar box with a built-in foot stand.

Luxe Leather Photo Wallet

www.aspinaloflondon.com

Croc embossed or calfskin leather album with tab closure to show off up to forty photos of the family. Comes in a variety of colors and textures.

Stylish Travel Case

www.stephaniejohnson.com

Moms who travel will love this stylish Stephanie Johnson ML Traveler travel case with three inside pouches, mirror snap-out, and plastic lining.

Pretty Tissue Covers

www.lekkerhome.com

Why is it moms are always ready with a Kleenex? Now she can pull one out of a portable yet swanky Alice Tissue Holder.

Bayou Classic Turkey Fryer Kit

www.BBQguys.com 🎁🎁🎁

No holiday will ever be the same once Dad gets going with this turkey fryer. This thirty-quart Fryer Kit comes with a basket, pot, and everything he needs to get that turkey fried.

Concert Tickets

www.ticketmaster.com prices vary

See what's coming to their town and get them a pair of tickets for a night out on you.

Photo Locket Key Ring

www.exposuresonline.com 🎁

Moms love this stuff. Every time they leave the house, they get to take you with them. Locket is also engravable.

World Poker Tournament Boot Camp

www.wptbootcamp.com 🎁🎁🎁🎁 (check site for tour stops)

An exciting two-day, hands-on event where students will be tutored on all aspects of competitive, tournament, Texas Hold 'Em Poker from some of the greatest minds of the World Poker Tour today.

Photo Handbag

www.ebags.com 🎁🎁🎁+

They can have their favorite photos on them at all times with a Gina Alexander photo handbag. Made of bridal satin fabric, some designs also have metal feet, leather trim, and leather handles.

Personalized Puzzles

www.puzzlemaker.com (part of discovery.com) free

Create an original book of puzzles—crossword puzzle, word search, cryptogram, and more—that only you and the recipient know the answers to.

Vacation Package

www.aa.com and www.continental.com prices vary

Send them on the vacation they should have taken years ago. Most major airlines sell gift cards that can be redeemed for flights, hotels, cars, or entire vacation packages. Put as much money as you want onto the card (increments and maximums vary by airline) and send them on a vacation of their dreams.

The Mom and Dad TV Blanket

www.plumparty.com 🎁🎁

Here's a way to be even lazier while watching TV. The Polarfleece Ultimate TV Blanket features a deep foot pocket and handy accessories pocket for remote control, book, reading glasses, and anything else that needs to be stored. "Mom" is embroidered on a periwinkle blanket, and "Dad" is embroidered on a gray one.

Car Wash Kit

www.topoftheline.com 🎁🎁

This well-stocked car wash kit comes with every accessory you can imagine to get the cleanest car on the block: nozzles, brushes, squeegees, and more.

Photo Tie

www.personalcreations.com 🎁

It appears to be a regular tie, but upon closer inspection, he'll notice that a personal photo creates the pattern.

Cosmo Girl Shower Wrap and Spa Products Gift Set

www.thepajamastore.com 🎁🎁🎁

The perfect gift to pamper your mama. Gift set comes with a Cosmo Girl chenille shower wrap with Velcro fastener, Pomegranate Fig body butter with shea butter and jojoba oil, a Pomegranate Fig bath soak made up of organic white tea, Dead Sea salts, botanical extracts, and moisturizing essential oils.

Classic Car Replica

www.franklinmint.com 🎁🎁+

Pick your year, make, and model and give Dad a mini version of some of the world's classic cars. Each handcrafted piece comes with background information on the special details of that car.

Alan "First American in Space" Shepard Autograph

www.thespaceshop.com 🎁🎁🎁🎁🎁

Alan Shepard was the first American to journey into space on May 5, 1961. The Kennedy Space Center offers this official Alan Shepard collection that displays his authentic signature along with two mission patches, two bronze mission coins, two 8 × 10 photographs, and an engraved information nameplate. The items are presented in a 16 × 28 gold frame with double matting.

World Globe and Stand

www.shiptheweb.com 🎁🎁🎁🎁

This forty-eight-inch-high Replogle Continental Globe is a raised-relief globe with parchment-colored oceans. It's cradled in a simplistic wrought-iron stand that will easily go with any type of décor.

Elegant Tea

www.teaforte.com 🎁

Tea forte teas are hand-cut whole tea leaves in a silken pyramid-shaped infuser. Some of the unique gourmet flavors include black currant, citrus mint, and lemon ginger.

Plaid Monogrammed Cosmetics Bags

www.objectsofdesireinc.com 🎁🎁/large

Made from 100 percent dupioni silk, these luxurious and brightly colored cosmetics bags come in a variety of plaid and sport a single personalized initial. Each bag is lined in vinyl and zips closed.

Iitalla Toikka Glass Birds

www.fitzsu.com 🎁🎁🎁+

Each of these delicate little birds is made of hand-blown glass by Iittala, a Finnish company. Designed by Oiva Toikka, these birds are elegant additions to a bookshelf.

Eyeglass Coaster

www.decorativethings.com 🎁

You will never lose your eyeglasses again with this stylish plastic eyeglass tray around. Twenty-four fabric prints to choose from.

Leather Wine Carrier

www.treasuresworldwide.com 🎁🎁

This is the Cadillac of wine carriers. The Royce Leather Wine Presentation Case holds two bottles of wine in a suede-lined, padded interior. The case has a zip-around design, a sturdy carrying handle, and a hang tag that can be imprinted or personalized. Comes in black, coco, or tan leather.

Customized Sterling Silver Cuff

www.elsewares.com 🎁🎁/eight characters (pricing increases with more characters)

Elegantly simple, a customized sterling silver bracelet cuff by GK Designs can be hand-stamped to say anything you want it to say.

Ties for Every Subject

www.customties.com 🎁🎁

Pick your topic, and you'll find a tie that features it as part of the Museum Artifacts theme ties collection. From a Civil War battle map to holiday themed to beer to pets, the ties are all 100 percent silk and fully lined.

Mom and Dad Mugs

www.ournameismud.com 🎁/each

These hand-painted ceramic mugs say "M is for Mom . . . Not Maid" and "D is for Dad . . . Not Dough"—reiterating what they've said for years.

All-Clad BBQ Set

www.chefsresource.com 🎁🎁🎁

This gourmet grilling tool set comes with a two-pronged fork, marinating brush, locking tongs, and turner. Tools are all 18/10 stainless steel and come housed in a hard-sided protective case.

A Stay at a Bed-and-Breakfast

www.bedandbreakfast.com prices vary

Send the folks off on a romantic weekend. This site offers B and B gift certificates that are accepted at over 3,500 B and Bs around the United States.

THE QUIRKY PAL

The Quirky Pals have talents no one else has mastered and ideas you wish were your own. Like when they wallpapered their living room with a digital mural close-up of their own eye or bought themselves a year's subscription to the Bacon-of-the-Month Club. Nothing is too outrageous for these friends; in fact, the weirder, the better. So you run no risk giving something as unusual as a belt with your smiling faces emblazoned on the buckle. Tickets to Doug Henning's Magical Comeback Tour would make the perfect outing. And don't rule out distasteful T-shirts that make people gasp. The quirky pals are unconventional and weird—even embarrassing at times—but you admire them for flaunting originality in an oftentimes uninspired world.

$100 Bill Toilet Paper

www.justtoiletpaper.com 🎁/roll

Ever dreamed of wiping with some Benjamins? They'll feel like a real playa with this toilet paper printed with the image of hundred dollar bills.

A Sweet Lid

www.hartfordyork.com 🎁🎁+

What sort of hat would they wear? A beret . . . a porkpie . . . a Greek fisherman? Choose from loads of styles.

Portrait Stationery Set

www.shout-outstationery.com 🎁🎁🎁 (one person in image) + $60 for a full stationery set

It's personalized notes to the next level. Send in a photo of yourself, and professional illustrators will draw your likeness and it will be printed on colorful stationery. Set includes stationery, note cards, notepads, and return address labels.

Librarian Action Figure

www.mcphee.com 🎁

Don't you want to own an action figure modeled after a real-life librarian (Nancy Pearl from the Seattle area)? Press a button, and her arm will move to "Shush."

Bruce the Sock Monkey

www.bruceandfriends.com 🎁/box of eight cards

Bruce is a model sock monkey; he poses in colorful photographs solo and with monkey buds for a special series of note cards.

Garden Gnome Plant Stakes

www.patinastores.com 🎁

Just 4" high, these cute plant stakes will keep a garden company.

Unusual Photos

www.davinaz.com 🎁🎁+

Photographer Davina Zagury adopts orphaned dolls and doll parts and captures their beauty on film. They're sad and lonely, but someone loves them.

Wonder Woman Undie Set

www.webundies.com 🎁

Just like your old underoos . . . but these days they're worn under business suits.

Crystal Ball

www.samadhicushions.com 🎁🎁🎁🎁

Six-inch crystal ball with stand allows your pal to channel the other side.

Stylish Leg Warmers

www.sock-dreams.com 🎁+

Pull them to your knees or scrunch them around your ankles; they'll keep your calves snug and warm. Leg warmers come in all sizes and materials.

Word Tees

www.hottopic.com 🎁

The more cynical quirky pals will appreciate these T-shirts with sulky sayings like "I ❤ Revenge" or "Disgruntled Employee of the Month."

UndergroundToys

www.kidrobot.com 🎁+

Kid Robot has a huge inventory of underground toys and collectibles from Japan and the West. You'll find Gloomy

Bears, Urban Vinyl Toys, Capsule Toys, Designer Plush Toys, and more.

'80s T-shirt

www.80stees.com 🎁+

Choose from a huge selection of music, movie, or TV homages. You can find a tee that reads "I Love Jake Ryan" from *Sixteen Candles*, or "The Italian Stallion" from *Rocky*, or one with the *Fraggle Rock* characters, or musical ones celebrating bands like Ratt and Styx.

Maggot Necklace

www.bittersweetsny.com 🎁🎁🎁

The solid-silver maggot dangling off a necklace shows off a person's sunnier side.

Retro Chocolate Bars

www.chocolatebarnyc.com 🎁

Imagine a chocolate bar filled with Malt Ball or Key Lime Pie or Salty Pretzel. Retro Bar gift set comes packaged in a nifty eight-bar sampler.

Blazing Fire DVD

www.plasmawindow.com 🎁

Hit Play on the TV, and suddenly there's a roaring fire in their living room.

Personalized Belts

www.nicnorman.com 🎁🎁🎁

Custom design a belt buckle starting with a photograph; choose size, shape, and style of the buckle and the belt.

Chocolate Face

www.chocolographyboutique.com 🎁

Put a favorite photo on a piece of chocolate. Chocolate is designed to look like a framed portrait, 9½" × 5½".

Offensive T-Shirts

www.tshirthell.com 🎁

Some really funny and obnoxious T-shirts you'll have a hard time finding in a store.

Personalized Paper Dolls

www.paperkids.com 🎁🎁

They look super real—paper dolls customized to look like a person in a photo. Send in a shot, and each Paper Kids set comes with the paper person on sturdy paper stock to cut out, plus eight to ten cutout outfits and accessories.

Chocolate Tea

www.harney.com 🎁/8 oz.

Not your mother's teas . . . try chocolate-flavored loose tea.

Scenic Mural

www.blueriverdigital.com 🎁/square foot

Plaster a wall with images like a tropical beach scene, mountain panorama, breathtaking sunset, vibrant cityscape, and more.

Tampon Case

www.uncommongoods.com 🎁🎁

It's time tampons made a style statement. Choose from several sassy and sleek case styles.

Customized Nikes

www.nikeid.com 🎁🎁+

Customize a funky pair of Nike sneaks from scratch with the Nike ID program.

Bacon-Scented Air Freshener

www.mcphee.com 🎁

This Bacon Air Freshener will make a room smell like Sunday brunch 24-7. Can also get a meat one shaped like a T-bone that smells like barbecue.

Colored Wigs

www.bewild.com 🎁

Pick a color—any color—and head out for the night.

Rocky Horror Trivia Game

www.bettysattic.com 🎁🎁

If they're not brave enough to hop up onstage, there's still a way for them to show off their *Rocky Horror Picture Show* knowledge. The Rocky Horror Trivia Game will either pose over 1,200 trivia questions, or they can roll a die and act out the characters. Score points as you go.

Fantasy Jewelry

www.fantasyjewelrybox.com 🎁+

Want a gorgeous diamond ring but don't have the cash? Fantasy Jewelry Box sells an assortment of costume jewelry that doesn't look like a costume. The designs try to replicate delicate and authentic rings, earrings, and more.

Cardboard Bush

www.hollywoodmegastore.com

Order a life-sized cardboard cutout of our president. President George W. Bush stands at six feet and is ready to defend his administration.

Clown Nesting Dolls

www.mcphee.com

This set of five nesting dolls features a collection of clowns that get progressively more evil as they get smaller. The biggest is an unassuming goofy clown, but by the time you're down to the smallest, it's just a straight-up devil.

Freeze-Dried Spaghetti Dinner

www.thespaceshop.com

This authentic space meal is just like the ones real astronauts eat while on a mission. Meal includes spaghetti with meat sauce, ice cream, and strawberries.

Bacon-of-the-Month Club

www.mightygoods.com

Twelve different artisan bacons are sent out along with a bacon T-shirt, a pig ballpoint pen, and more.

NASA Flight Suit

www.thespaceshop.com

This adult-sized blue space flight suit is an exact replica of what astronauts wear up into space. Made of 65 percent cotton, 35 percent polyester, and straight from the Kennedy Space Center.

Beef Jerky Club

www.jerky-of-the-month.com 🎁🎁

Know someone who loves beef jerky? Sign them up for the Jerky-of-the-Month Club. For six months, they'll receive a four-ounce package of beef jerky in a new and exciting flavor.

Restored Vintage Phone

www.artthang.com 🎁🎁🎁🎁

Go retro with an authentic phone from the '20s, '30s, or '40s that's been fully restored and is operational. The ring even sounds like the old days.

Needlepoint Disco Lady Pillow

www.jonathanadler.com 🎁🎁🎁🎁

Needlepoint gets a makeover with this pillow, 16" × 16" with a feather/down insert, that gives a big shout out to the riotous days of disco. Get down!

Tribal Tattoo Sleeves

www.sleevesclothing.com 🎁🎁🎁

Short-sleeved T-shirt with long sheer fabric sleeves attached that are designed to look like you have real inked appendages.

Animal Pillow

www.velocityartanddesign.com 🎁🎁+

Cuddle up with a friendly duck, fawn, and other creatures and critters. Salvor Fauna Pillows feature a photograph of an animal on a pillow that's shaped to the photo. Pillow is 100 percent cotton canvas silk-screened with water-based inks.

Glass Stiks

www.whatisblik.com 🎁/pack

Ordinary glass is more exciting when it's personalized with some colorful decals. Peel and stick to anything from drinking glasses to windows, and you have a whole new look. Decals are dishwasher safe and easily removable.

Morbid Socks

www.soxtogo.com 🎁

These socks say more than you need; they sport an image of a rifle and the saying "I'm gonna kill something."

Painted Antique Wood Shoe Form

www.artthang.com 🎁🎁

It's an odd but eye-catching gift to give: an authentic women's shoe form is dressed up with an artistic paint job to make a lovely household accessory.

Jell-O Shots Kit

www.bewild.com 🎁

The Shell-o-Jots Kit comes with twelve plastic shot glasses, lemon and cherry flavored shell-o-jots, and a recipe book.

Chinese Take-Out Lamp

www.wrapables.com 🎁

It looks like a Chinese food take-out box—it even has a wire handle and comes with chopsticks—but it's a lamp. Made of heat-resistant paper.

Telephone Handset for Your Cell Phone

www.mxyplyzyk.com

A regular telephone handset that plugs into your cell phone earpiece jack.

Eggling

www.catfishgreetings.com

A plant that hatches out of an eggshell! It's actually a porous porcelain eggshell, and when you crack off the top, there's soil and a seed pack. Choose from among thyme, mint, basil, and Italian parsley.

Smart-Ass Panties

www.cocoacrayon.com

Let their butt do the talking. These thongs have sassy comments on the back such as "Desperate Housewife" and "ooh la la."

Spazzstick

www.chemicalevolution.com

Cure chapped lips and get a boost of energy at the same time. The Spazzstick is a new lip balm that's loaded with caffeine. Comes in mint or vanilla toffee.

Crime-Scene Kit

www.plumparty.com

They will freak someone out with this realistic crime-scene kit. It comes with white chalk, yellow evidence markers, and a one-hundred-foot roll of "Caution: Crime Scene" tape.

THE JET-SETTER

The Jet-Setters have more frequent-flier miles than most people have earned in their lifetimes. They know details like where to get a massage in the Madrid Airport to what flights leave New York for London after eight p.m. The Jet-Setters travel the world, and they do it in style. Which may leave you jealous and resentful at times, but there's a way around that. When it's time to get the Jet-Setters something, live vicariously, and pretend *you're* the one taking off for Tokyo. Ask yourself what you'd want on your journey. Love music? Choose from a number of sleek portable stereo options. If you dream of comfort and convenience on your trip, there's no end to travel-friendly pampering paraphernalia and culture-crossing tools. Or if you know you'll want to preserve the wonderful memories once you get home, think about how you can turn those special snapshots into personal Picassos. Half of the fun of jet-setting is getting ready to go, so enjoy that part of the ride, and take notes for when it's your turn to hit the road.

Automatic Plant Waterer

www.travelproducts.com 🎁

A lifesaver for any traveler, the Rain-Maid automatic planter waterer takes care of the greens when no one's home. Once the reservoir is filled with water and placed in the plant, it will release water once every three and a half days for up to two weeks.

Book Safe

www.kopes.com 🎁

As long as the burglars don't read, it's not a bad idea to hide valuables in a real book with a secret compartment. They'll never find the diamonds there!

Travel Bar for Two

www.uncommongoods.com 🎁🎁

It's always happy hour with this sleek and sophisticated Mini Travel Bar. The set is equipped with sleek, stainless steel bar tools and a flask and comes in a nifty and sturdy leather and canvas carrying case.

WonderVase

www.magellans.com 🎁

They can brighten up a hotel room with the WonderVase. It packs flat and molds to any shape to hold fresh flowers anywhere in the world. Set includes one in each size: small, medium, and large.

Luxurious Travel Pillowcase

www.threadcountzzz.com 🎁

Airplane pillows can get a little scary when you think of who else has used them. So give a personal pillowcase to ensure they've got a layer of protection. And it doesn't hurt that it's made of an ultrahigh thread count, 100 percent Egyptian cotton sateen fabric.

Sachet Stack

www.casualelegance.com 🎁🎁

These A Touch of Ivy sachets are great for a personal fragrance on the road. The stack is boxed, tied with a bow, and is gift-ready.

Stylish Shoe Bags

www.hattiemayfield.com 🎁

For more organized (and clean) travel, they can use these shoe bags in stylish fabric choices to protect their suitcase contents.

"Places to Remember" Leather Notebook

www.smythson.com 🎁🎁🎁🎁

A hardbound notebook in red or black leather is a classy way for them to jot down their favorite parts of the trip.

Disposable Bathing Suits

www.fredala.com 🎁

One size fits all. This bathing suit is made from an unfinished stretch fabric that has been laser cut. Helps lighten the load to toss out on the road.

Food from Around the World

www.earthy.com 🎁🎁+

Not quite the same as eating it in the real country, but this gourmet food provider has gift baskets themed by country. Spain basket ($89) includes saffron, Extra Virgin Arbequina olive oil, smoked paprika, Calasparra mountain-grown paella rice, capers, anchovies, roasted piquillo pimientos, marcona almonds in rosemary honey, fig and almond cake, and old-world-style quince paste. Arrives packed in an attractive hand-woven basket.

On the Move Survival Travel Kit

www.relaxdepot.com 🎁🎁

Designed for people on the go, this Oscar + Dehn Eye 3-Step Eye Kit for travelers has a thermal gel eye mask, two essential oils to calm, and eye gel to soothe.

Capture a Special Sight

www.canvasondemand.com 🎁🎁+

Turn a digital still of their favorite photo from their travels into a work of art on canvas. Choose between photorealistic or treated to look like an oil painting ($29 extra).

Travel Magazine Subscription

www.amazon.com 🎁/year

Order a yearlong magazine subscription to a travel magazine like *Condé Nast Traveler*—something that will help them plan for the next adventure.

Leather Jewelry Roll

www.daisyarts.com 🎁🎁🎁🎁

A luscious leather roll with suede interior comes equipped with three zipper pockets, a ring strap with snaps on either side for easy access, and one 7" snap closure pocket.

iPod Speakers

http://store.apple.com

Rock the room with the SonicImpact i-Fusion portable speakers for the iPod. Aside from amazing sound quality, it has a hardcover case for protection while traveling and a storage compartment for your iPod. Built-in docking station for recharging.

Talking Dictionary/Translator

www.ectaco.com

Select an English phrase on the Lingo Pacifica Talk Multi-language Translator TR-2203, and you'll hear a prerecorded translation in one of ten languages. The device has a vocabulary of 200,000 words and 23,000 practical phrases.

Travel Candles

www.startreatment.com

Basket of twelve uniquely scented travel candles are perfect for the road.

Ferrari Travel Clock

www.ferraristore.com

Not only does the Silverstone alarm clock tell you the date and display the indoor temperature, but it wakes you up to an alarm featuring a Ferrari revving its engine.

Portable Travel Smoke Detector

www.corporatetravelsafety.com

Just because the United States requires them doesn't mean the rest of the world does. This small, lightweight lifesaver is easy to bring along on a trip. Runs on a nine-volt battery.

Black-and-White Single-Use Camera

www.ritzcamera.com 🎁

Maybe they've always dreamed of being a famous photographer known for capturing the mood with stylish black-and-white photos. Now they have their chance with a Kodak disposable black-and-white camera.

Tumi Flow Flight Bag

www.tumi.com 🎁🎁🎁

Heavy water-resistant fabric is a stylish unisex carry-on bag. It features multiple compartments including phone pocket, water bottle holder, and cord port.

Stylish Luggage Tags

www.dafridge.com 🎁

A Lugtagz colorful luggage tag makes traveling much easier. Bonus: if the plane goes down, the tags are waterproof and fireproof.

Traveler's Key Chain

www.fortunoff.com 🎁

This small sterling silver key chain features an airplane on one end and a screw-off globe on the other. Remove globe to add keys. Great item for when a traveler needs a place to put their keys.

Light-Up Magnifier

www.brookstone.com 🎁

Need to check the map but it's too dark? This handy Lighted Pop Up 2× Magnifier will help them find where they're going and light the way.

Travel Air Purifier

www.protravelgear.com 🎁🎁🎁

Airplane air is not the cleanest; there are colds floating around just waiting to be caught. Now it's possible to purify your personal breathing space with the Mini Mate Travel Air Purifier. Weighing less than two ounces, this device hangs from a strap around your neck and offers a powerful purifying system.

No Jet Lag

www.letravelstore.com 🎁

A natural way to relieve jet lag, these chewable tablets are made of five botanical ingredients.

Itty Bitty Book Light—Travel Edition

www.zelco.com 🎁🎁

This lightweight portable book light clips to any book and provides light to read anywhere, anytime. Comes in a carrying case.

Satin Shoe Stuffers

www.giftdistrict.com 🎁🎁

Keep those pointy-toe shoes in tip-top form with lavender-scented shoe stuffer sachets in white, red, blue, black, gold, or pink satin.

Pack EZ Set

www.packhappy.com 🎁🎁/set

This set of three brightly colored bags are printed and designed to keep your travel essentials in order: Green for your shoes, orange for your wash, fuchsia for your undies.

Each bag is made of stretchy bengaline fabric with a drawstring closure.

"Follow Me" Electronic Monitoring System

www.hometreats.com

Attach the signal transmitter to any valuable—purse, laptop, small child—and carry the tiny receiver, which will beep as soon as your valuables are more than fifteen feet away. Comes with one signal transmitter, one key chain receiver, rechargeable base, and an AC adapter.

Hok2 Squeeze and Shave Travel Razors

www.enkueros.net

A traveler's must-have for smooth skin, this travel razor set is a razor and shaving cream in one. The travel pack comes with three disposable blades, three squeeze tubes of shaving cream, and an attachment sleeve. Scents are Whole Wheat Protein, Natural Plant Extract, and Ocean Botanical.

Graphic Image Traveler's Atlas

www.katespaperie.com

Only 4.5" × 6", this compact world atlas is bound in calfskin and focuses on cities, transportation, and points of interest; 320 pages with gilt edges.

Geography Pillow

www.tabulatua.com

Color throw pillows by Cat Studio Geography measure 19" × 19" and feature hand-embroidered original designs that celebrate American states and cities, and foreign countries.

iLingo—English to Euro Pack

http://store.apple.com

If they already have an iPod, this translation pack software is easily added. The iLingo program translates over 450 words and phrases from English to French, German, Italian, and Spanish. The word is displayed on the screen, then pronounced out loud with the push of a button.

Paddywax Destination Candle

www.paddywax.com +

These luxurious candles evoke the scents of some of the most exotic places in the world: Provence, Tuscany, Sahara, Tahiti, Mikonos, and Bordeaux. Available in various shapes and sizes.

World Travel Adapter

www.flight001.com

The World Travel Adapter from Swiss Travel Products is a single adapter that contains options for more than 150 countries. Adapter does not convert voltage!

Passport/Document Case

www.flight001.com

Travel in style with a fashionable and colorful microfiber passport and document case.

THE MELANCHOLY MATE

It could have been the unexpected breakup. Or that bitch of a boss. Or the sudden appearance of an extra thirty pounds. You've all been there from time to time, so you know it's hopeless, really, trying to convince the Melancholy Mate to crack a smile. Nothing you could ever say would make them feel better, right? Well, save your breath, because times like these call for emergency action. It's your responsibility to distract your saddened pals from their misery and get them focused on something more positive! Help them find a cosmic peace with an inspirational mantra to put their lives in perspective. Get them to laugh with a ridiculous gag gift; fake poop was invented for times like these. Or, in a really bad case of the blues, encourage them to give their systems a shock and fling their bodies from an airplane. Nobody likes being depressed, so it's up to you to remind them of what life's like under sunny skies.

Lemon Tree

www.napastyle.com 🎁🎁🎁

What better way to turn lemons into lemonade: start with the real deal. The Meyer lemon tree fruits most of the year, is easy to keep alive, and brings a bit of brightness to someone's life.

Tranquility Fountain

www.redenvelope.com 🎁🎁

Bring peace and tranquility to a room with a rock fountain and the sound of trickling water.

Possession Protector

www.psychicgirl.com 🎁🎁

Blessed by a real psychic, these spiritual charms are supposed to ward off evil.

Shiatsu Massaging Pillow

www.brookstone.com 🎁🎁🎁

Unload worries as this deep kneading shiatsu pillow massager kneads troubles away with targeted acupressure on your head and neck.

Fancy Leather Journal

www.jennibick.com 🎁🎁🎁 (6 × 8)

Handmade distressed Italian leather journal with handmade paper from the Amalfi Coast holds 160 pages of acid-free paper—perfect for getting it all out.

Soothing Coloring Book

www.uncommongoods.com 🎁

This exclusive coloring book should calm their minds.

Peaceful images of shapes and landscapes are ready to be colored in.

Happy Mind Aromatherapy Diffuser Gift Set

www.saffronrouge.com 🎁

The smiling happy face should put anyone in a good mood. This pocket diffuser in a tin and aromatherapy scents of grapefruit and rose geranium will lift saddened spirits.

Teddy Bear-Gram

www.vermontteddybear.com 🎁🎁+

Box contains a handmade Vermont Teddy Bear, along with chocolates or caramels and a card with a special note. Bear can be personalized with a name.

Self-Affirming Tank Top

www.webundies.com 🎁

Black tank with a perfect motto to cheer someone up and put life in perspective: "It's All About Me" is branded across their chest.

Therapy Flash Cards

www.uncommongoods.com 🎁

Lighten the mood and turn their pain into a game with these flash cards. Each has a term on one side and the definition of the disorder on the back.

Tattoo

www.everytattoo.com prices vary

Shock them from their funk. You can include with the certificate a promise that you will be there to hold their hand. Some tattoo parlors offer body piercing services as well, so if you're not 100 percent sure of your recipient's preferences, but you know they'd be into a gift like this, find a parlor that offers both services and let them choose their pain. If you're not in the know, this site will name some parlors in your area.

Primordial Sound Meditation

www.chopra.com prices vary

Primordial Sound Meditation, as introduced by Dr. Deepak Chopra, is a mantra-based practice that systematically calms a person, allowing them to reach more peaceful levels of the mind. Dr. Chopra isn't considered a guru for nothing; his teachings may help your frowning friend find some focus. Go to the site to find a meditation instructor in your area.

Picture Frame Charm Bracelet

www.lillianvernon.com 🎁🎁

Remind them that they're loved. Fill each photo frame on this charm bracelet with a special image to make them smile.

Spa Trip

www.spafinder.com prices vary

Everyone deserves to be pampered; there's just a little less guilt when it's free! Treat them to anything from a manicure/pedicure, an aromatherapy massage, or a daylong spa package that could include a seaweed scrub down followed by a mud bath followed by a power wash. This search engine will help you find a spa in your area.

Framed Original Classic Record Albums

www.tunescompany.com 🎁🎁🎁

Maybe the sight of an original David Bowie *Changes* album will take them back to happier times. Authentic records come framed.

Guardian Angel Candle

www.mostlyangelsonline.com prices vary

This Guardian Angel of Joy & Happiness candle should bring some positive energy and good vibes into their lives. Other Guardian Angel Candles available.

Smiley Face Plush Doll

www.bitwisegifts.com 🎁

Hang this little guy anywhere, and he'll remind you to be happy.

Yoga Classes

www.yoga.com prices vary

They're forced to leave their stress at the door for ninety minutes and focus on themselves. This search engine will help you find a class in their area.

Instant Boyfriend

www.bitwisegifts.com 🎁

It's about time there was a hot, charming guy to adore them. The Instant Adoring Boyfriend DVD tells them what they deserve to hear.

Dedicate a Star

www.dedicateastar.com 🎁🎁

When a person's world is closing in, naming a star after

them may be the perfect reminder of how big the universe really is. The official National Star Association Register's Deluxe Dedication Kit includes a congratulatory letter, beautiful oak wooden frame and naming certificate, constellation star map, and a stylish certificate holder.

Broadway Show and Swag

www.broadwaynewyork.com prices vary

Show tunes therapy! Get someone tickets to a Broadway show, along with a souvenir for the show they're going to be seeing.

Send Them Skydiving

www.uspa.org prices vary

It's time they make that jump to move on emotionally and physically to the next place. Make sure the facility is certified with the United States Parachute Association (USPA). Check the site for some guidelines, information, and links to locations near you.

Men Are Such Fools Candle

www.plumparty.com 🎁

'Nuff said.

Voodoo Ritual Kit

www.voodooshop.com 🎁🎁

This Voodoo Ritual Kit comes straight from New Orleans. It comes with all you need to cast a voodoo spell: instructions, coffin box, voodoo doll, candle, potion oil, mini gris-gris, parchment paper, and incense. Pick your theme and start chanting.

Hire a Professional Organizer

www.napo.net prices vary

Hire some help in cleaning out the past. Professional organizers help individuals take control of their surroundings, time, papers, and their systems for life. They clear clutter and feng shui homes—a good way to start over. National Association of Professional Organizers search engine will help you find a certified organizer in your area.

Customize a Watch

www.ewatchfactory.com 🎁+

If they're watching time tick by, they might as well be looking at something special. Transfer any image to the face of a wristwatch and design everything from the style to the hands.

Remote Control Whoopee Cushion

www.alphabetsnyc.com 🎁

It's an easy laugh, but it's always a laugh.

Hugs and Kisses Pajama Gift Set

www.thepajamastore.com 🎁🎁🎁

This cotton PJs and slipper gift set have love written all over them. PJs by Cherry Pie are pink and white striped, and bottoms have a drawstring waist to fit all sizes. The slippers by Fanciful Soles are hand beaded with pink and red lips, and they're comfy, too.

"All Will Be Well" Votive

www.ournameismud.com 🎁

This dainty ceramic candle votive has the saying "All Will Be Well" hand painted around the rim.

Smiley Face Affirmation Ball

www.bitwisegifts.com

It works like a Magic 8 Ball, but the Smiley Face Affirmation Ball showers you with compliments instead of answers. Sayings like "Have you lost weight?" and "Your breath is so minty" will guarantee to make anyone who's down in the dumps feel a little better.

Heart Artbox

www.artboxproject.com

A number of artists were invited to design images for this project where their artwork is turned into lamps and illuminated. The boxes are 8" × 8" × 3", operate on a plug and a switch, and can be hung on a wall or sit on a shelf. Vacide Erda-Zimic's Heart box design is a perfect pick-me-up. Each artbox comes packaged in a gift box and includes a low-wattage bulb.

Zen Sense Gift Set

www.maroma-usa.com

The Leaf Garden Zen Sense Gift Set features three peaceful fragrances: Bamboo, Green Tea, and Alpine Cedar. Each box contains two meditation votives, three sachets, twenty-four incense leaves, one handmade stone incense holder, and one handmade scroll featuring a garden haiku.

Quotable Mug

www.quotablecards.com

Fourteen-ounce ceramic mug will provide inspiration with every sip. Choose from among two dozen quotes including: "Go confidently in the direction of your dreams! Live the life you've imagined."—*Thoreau*

Quotable Canvas

www.quotablecards.com

Inspirational quotes on canvas stretched on a thick wood frame will keep your pal thinking positive thoughts. Examples include "Life isn't about finding yourself, it's about creating yourself," and "What would you attempt to do if you knew you could not fail?" Each square canvas measures 10" × 10" × 1.5".

Detox in a Box

www.vickerey.com

The do-it-yourself Detox Kit comes with everything you need to go through a detox cleansing at home. Created by holistic physician Mark Hyman, M.D., co-medical director at Canyon Ranch in the Berkshires, the process is designed to remove toxins and allergens, boost immunity, and restore energy levels. Kit comes with an instruction manual, assessment questionnaires, two informative CDs, and seventy easy-to-follow flash cards.

"You Are Loved" Mug

www.ournameismud.com

Ceramic mug with "You Are Loved" painted on it. Perfect for someone who needs that little reminder.

Hand-Painted Themed Martini Glasses

www.sbceramicstore.com

Lolita's groovy themed martini glasses make a much-needed cocktail hour more fun! Each hand-painted glass holds seven ounces of a tasty martini and is decorated with images and a recipe to suit a specific theme. There are over forty themes to choose from like Bikini Martini, Pokertini Martini, Glamourtini Martini, and Chocolatini Martini.

100 Simple Secrets of Happy People

www.barnesandnoble.com 🎁

This book has taken scientific research and translated it to one hundred practices, attitudes, and habits for happiness. Each tip is accompanied by a story that tells you how people have put that advice to use. It makes happiness look so easy!

Tony Robbins CD Set

www.tonyrobbins.com 🎁🎁🎁🎁

For over twenty-five years, Tony Robbins has been motivating people around the world by sharing his tools and strategies for achievement and fulfillment. Tony's *Get the Edge* ten-CD set teaches you how to maximize energy, create better relationships, train yourself to better balance your emotions, and more. Set also comes with an instructional video and a personal journal.

Mrs. Fields Basket of Smiles

www.mrsfields.com 🎁🎁

One dozen of Mrs. Fields smiley face butter cookie cutouts in a gift basket should make anyone feel happy.

Ice Cream of the Month Club

www.icecreamsource.com 🎁🎁/month

Each month, they'll receive four new pints of selected ice cream flavors. Select any number of months.

Chez Bella Kit Kat House

www.bellabeauty.net 🎁🎁

Bella Beauty's Kit Kat House has a fluffy pink boa, along with Minty Lip Gloss, Crème Blush Cheek Stick, Roller Ball Eye Shadow, and Shimmer Powder Poof, all in a cheerful girly canister.

THE NEW EXEC

They finally made it. To the New Execs, school is a thing of the past, and the future holds nothing but opportunities. It's taken their determination, sacrifice, and good old-fashioned grit to make it here; that metal plate with their name on it didn't come easy. As they settle into their new corporate lifestyle, there are some obvious ways to congratulate them on this achievement. You can help establish their new authoritative style with executive threads from a reputable store. Embellish them with an expensive electronic item they can't otherwise afford (yet). Provide them with an amusing toy distraction for when they need to come up for air. The New Execs have entered the real world now, and whatever you can do to smooth this momentous transition will be appreciated. Now if you can just figure out how to get them a promotion . . .

Tie Bar

www.tiffany.com

Classy men pin their ties with a sterling silver tie bar from Tiffany's Atlas Collection.

Napa Leather Manila Envelope

www.giftsforprofessionals.com

Forget the boring yellowed manila envelope to carry work documents. A Florentine Napa leather one with a string closure for 8.5" × 11" docs has more class.

Executive Hammock

www.shopexit9.com

Power nap in this full-size executive hammock.

Dumb Dares for the Workplace

www.uncommongoods.com

They should be working, but this is more fun. Watch as they spin the Dare Selector and proceed to carry out some of the most ridiculous office dares ever. Game offers up 250 ways to harass your colleagues.

Amenity's On the Go Grooming Set

www.getamenity.com

Shaving set includes travel sizes of everything an exec needs for a clean shave on the road: brush, cream, aftershave, cleanser, and moisturizer.

Desktop Air Purifier

www.sharperimage.com

Office air is to be avoided if possible; they can stay healthy with a desktop air purifier. The Ionic Breeze Tabletop Silent Air Purifier is proven to reduce airborne allergens and irritants including dust mite allergens, pet dander, and cigarette smoke.

Nylon Canvas Tech Field Bag

www.katespade.com 🎁🎁🎁🎁

Stylish nylon bag has a Velcro closure, adjustable shoulder straps, exterior zipper pocket for audio and cellular, with an audio port for headphones. Bag is water-resistant.

Special Fortune Cookies

www.goodfortunes.com 🎁🎁/pail of twenty-five cookies

Wish them luck with a pail of classic fortune cookies dipped in chocolate.

Coffee/Tea-of-the-Month Club

www.coffeebean.com 🎁+

The Coffee Bean and Tea Leaf chain offers coffee/tea-of-the-month clubs—three- or six-month "passports" where you receive a different coffee or tea to try out each month.

Custom Photo NoteCube

www.exposuresonline.com 🎁

They'll think of you every time they take a note. Six hundred sheets per cube.

Desktop Garden

www.flaxart.com 🎁

Bring a bit of nature into the office with a Zen-like garden. Kit includes two resin architectural vases, tray, gravel, grass seed, and miracle soil for easy growth.

Rearview Computer Mirror

www.spoonsisters.com 🎁

They'll never have to worry about the boss walking up behind them. This convex mirror gives a wide-angle view of their surroundings.

The Slim Computer Case

www.acmemade.com 🎁🎁🎁

The Acme Made Slim case fits most laptop computers and is stylish to boot. Minimalist in structure, it has top grain leather handles, quilted satin lining, water-resistant ballistic nylon, and a one-year warranty.

Brooks Brothers Cuff Links

www.brooksbrothers.com 🎁🎁🎁

The Repp Stripe Cuff Link in sterling silver makes the suit.

Business Card Wallet

www.levenger.com 🎁🎁

The smart leather Card Wallet is made of smooth, full-grain leather and holds up to fifty business cards. Comes in toffee, black, or red.

Corporate Office Cube Doll Set

www.mcphee.com 🎁

Create an original bitter office space. Each set has one 2¾" posable plastic figure and all the necessary plastic parts to build a classic corporate cube: four walls, desk, chair, file cabinet, in/out-box, phone, and computer. Comes with a sticker sheet of decor for the cube. Site has features like downloadable office decorations and job title generator. Five different sets available.

Working Girl's Survival Kit

www.wishingfish.com

Never be caught in a pinch again at work. This kit comes with every emergency item imaginable: toothbrush, toothpaste, dental floss, lip balm, mints, pain reliever, hand lotion, emery board, nail clipper, clear nail polish, nail polish remover, hair brush, mirror, deodorant, tampons, lint remover, mending kit, stain remover, static remover, shoe shine wipes, Band-Aids, and tissues.

Personalized Paperweights

www.iomoi.com

Heavy glass oval paperweights display the owner's initials along with a specially selected design. Choose from over twenty-five distinct styles for men and women.

Alligator Cigar Case

www.bellatoff.com

To be broken out on special occasions, this brown alligator cigar case holds up to three cigars.

Burberry Plaid Tie

www.neimanmarcus.com

The man knows his plaids; the Novacheck tie is Burberry's signature design.

Amusing Desktop Sign

www.unusualthings.biz

This desktop sign collection is shaped like a desk nameplate, but you have a choice of thirty humorous sayings to display. Try "In a Meeting, the Practical Alternative to

Work." Or "Out to Lunch, and Short of a Sandwich." Each cardboard sign is 9" × 4¾".

Fashion Emergency Kit

www.seejanework.com

The last thing anyone wants to deal with at work is a wardrobe malfunction, so this Fashion Emergency Kit is there to help in a pinch. The tiny 3" × 3.5" kit comes with a sewing kit, a lint brush, double-stick tape, a black marker, and a booklet full of how to handle yourself in a fashion crisis.

Office on the Go

www.seejanework.com

If their job frequently takes them out of an office, this compact Office on the Go set comes with small versions of essential office supplies and includes scissors, a pen and pencil, tape, a stapler, and paper clips.

Leather Travel Valet

www.bloomingdales.com

This quality leather valet unsnaps to lay completely flat for packing. It's also lined in leather and available in red, blue, black, and saddle. Valet measures 5.25" × 5.25" × 1.75".

The Apprentice Donald Trump Talking Bobblehead

www.nbcuniversalstore.com

Just press a button and this 7" bobblehead of "The Donald" barks, "You're fired!" Perfect for the first day in a new office.

Crap Stamp

www.patinastores.com

It's one way to get fired; stamp up paperwork with a rubber stamp that says "I haven't got time to read this crap."

The Boss Toss

www.spoonsisters.com

When the boss becomes too much, load this trigger gun and launch a miniboss into space. Comes with gun and four bosses.

Sterling Silver Wallet Pen

www.spoonsisters.com

This wallet-sized sterling silver pen clips to the interior fold of a wallet without causing any extra bulk.

Whimsical Computer Mouse and Mouse Pad

www.sarut.com

These coordinated computer sets feature enchanting designs with coordinated images. Sure to lighten up any desk setting.

Miniature File Cabinet

www.giftsandgadgetsonline.com

This miniature 4.25" × 6" file cabinet organizes over seven hundred business cards. The top drawer has built-in digital clock with date. A–Z card index included.

The Massage Pen

www.thewritersedge.com

The Fisher Space Pen is pressurized to be able to write at any angle. But this version comes with a bonus built-in massager. Just press the round ball at the top of the pen to activate the vibrating massage, and it automatically turns into a more relaxing day at the office. Pen comes with a booklet that identifies stress points.

Cravat Multitie Hook

www.umbra.com

The chrome hanger holds multiple ties and hangs neatly over the top of a door.

Executive Pen Holder

www.wrapables.com

The electronic face on this Executive Pen Holder provides the date and time, temperature, daily alarm with snooze, countdown timer, birthday reminder, multiple musical tones—basically everything you need to keep you organized and on track with your schedule. Made of polished steel and black leather.

Office Dish Set

www.vessel-store.com

Plate, bowl, cup, and utensils all pack up together and are wrapped with a place mat.

Velour Computer Carrying Case

www.melissabeth.com

The Get Off My Case brightly colored computer cases make going to work more fun. The case features a velour exterior with leather trim and a contrasting pattern for the lining. The foam padding protects your computer from bangs. Comes in pink, robin's egg, camel, orchard green, navy blue, and heather grey.

Designer Letter Opener

www.retromodern.com 🎁🎁

Designed by Enzo Mari in 1962, this Ameland letter opener provides a fancy way to read the mail.

Executive Decision Maker

www.giftsforprofessionals.com 🎁

Spin the wheel, and you're directed to a decision: yes, no, maybe, today, tomorrow, sit on it, reorganize, and pass the buck.

Cartier Fountain Pen

www.worldlux.com 🎁🎁🎁🎁

Write in style with a Cartier Diabolo GT Fountain Pen. Comes in black with gold trim and features an 18k solid-gold nib.

Money Tree

www.smithandhawken.com 🎁+

Many Asian cultures believe that the money tree has the power to deliver wealth and good fortune. This five-stem braided money tree is easy to care for; it just needs a little bit of light and water. A medium-sized tree will reach about 3' high.

iPod Car System

http://store.apple.com 🎁🎁🎁

The Griffin Road Trip is the full package for a commuter who spends lots of time in a car. It transmits your iPod contents to a car radio using any FM frequency, plus comes with a cradle, and charger.

Bella Beauty Eye Essential Kit

www.bellabeauty.net

This tiny patent black box contains a mini mascara, kohl eyeliner, brow gel, and tweezers—a perfect touch-up kit for a girl on the go.

THE GOLDEN COUPLE

It's an age-old question: What's the secret to a lifelong marriage? How does a couple make it through fifty years of waking up to the same face every morning? Some couples will say it's knowing when to compromise. Others credit it to absolute and mutual trust. Still others say there's no explaining pure love. Indeed, to become a Golden Couple is quite a feat. You may think that the memories collected over the years aren't something that can be boxed and tied with a bow, but that's where you're wrong. What about dusting off those 16 mm home movies no one's watched in years and stage a grand rerelease? Or commemorate the generations this remarkable couple has spawned with an ornately decorated family tree? Better yet, give them everything they'd need for a private, intimate evening, and just leave them to their own devices. Don't put it past these lovebirds to keep it real—they've been doing it for half a century.

Historical Newspaper

www.newspaperarchive.com 🎁🎁

Commemorate a special day with an edition of a newspaper from that exact day. They'll get the full newspaper from a major U.S. city, along with a registered certificate of authenticity. Paper comes presented in leatherette binder personalized with the recipient's name and the newspaper name.

Photo Memory Quilt

www.calicocreekquilts.com 🎁🎁🎁🎁+

It's warmer than a photo album. Select from a number of designs displaying up to twenty-seven photos. Send in your photos, and they will be transferred to cloth and sewn into a handmade photo memory quilt straight from Arkansas.

Historic Tree

www.historictrees.com 🎁🎁

Share in a piece of botanical history. The American Forests Historic Tree Company ships saplings from some famous trees including the Lover's Live Oak, which descends from a 900-year-old tree in Brunswick, Georgia, where according to legend Indian braves courted maidens. Today, young lovers visit it for a blessing.

Gold-Dipped Roses

www.loveisarose.com 🎁🎁🎁🎁

Two actual 11" roses are preserved in 24k pure gold and presented in a Walnut Remembrance Box against black felt. Also in the box is a 2" × 3" engraved plate with a personal message for the golden couple.

Romantic Double Swing Set

www.porchswings.com 🎁🎁🎁🎁🎁

Made of sturdy cedar, the Great American Arbor Swing Set is built for two, hangs from a stand, and features a roof to shade the sun.

Floral Arrangement of Wedding Bouquet

www.marksflowers.com prices vary

Find a local florist and have them re-create a floral arrangement that mirrors the one the golden girl carried down the aisle.

Customized Nesting Dolls

www.thisisauto.com 🎁🎁🎁🎁🎁

Give a set of nesting dolls, each hand-painted in a family member's likeness. Just send in a photograph of each member to be included in the set. Choose from a set of three to five. Not cheap, but supercool.

Sweetheart Photo Cube

www.valentinesgifts.com 🎁

A 4.5" square cube features spots for four photographs and a choice of a love poem or the word "love" with a couple's customized names featured on one side. Comes in a natural-colored wood grain with engraving.

Hot Air Balloon Trip

www.ushotairballoon.com prices vary

Order a gift certificate from the United States Hot Air Balloon team for them, and they can redeem it at a location near them. This site will help you find a location.

Puppets of Them

www.puppetartists.com 🎁🎁🎁/puppet

Portrait puppets look just like them! Twenty-four inches tall with legs and twelve inches across from fingertip to fingertip.

Preserve Home Movies

www.yalefilmandvideo.com 🎁+

Transfer home movies to video. Based in L.A., Yale Film and Video will transfer any format to a digital master.

Professionally Drawn Family Tree

www.plaquemaker.com 🎁🎁🎁 + each name is $5

Have a hand-drawn, completely unique version of your family tree laser-engraved onto a solid 12" × 15" cherry plaque.

Platter Portrait of their Home

www.wirthsalander.com 🎁🎁🎁🎁

Send them a photo of the house, and they send you back a custom ceramic platter with your home portrait on it.

Vintage Magazine

www.vintagemagazines.com prices vary

Gallagher's Gallery and Archive in New York City will likely have the issue of *Time* magazine from the week they were married. They also carry everything from *Rolling Stone* to *Architectural Digest* to *Life* to *Vanity Fair.*

Greeting from the President

www.whitehouse.gov/greeting/ free

The President will sign a greeting to commemorate their fiftieth anniversary. Recipient must be a U.S. citizen to qualify. Go to the site for instructions on ordering.

Baccarat Crystal Heart

www.eluxury.com 🎁🎁🎁

This is what's kept them together for fifty years. The puffed red crystal heart by Baccarat is perfectly designed and colored.

Professional Portrait

www.mjkoza.com 🎁🎁🎁🎁🎁

Commission an artist to re-create their wedding photo in an oil painting portrait.

A Personalized Song

www.giftsongs.com 🎁🎁

Mark this momentous occasion with an original song composed especially for the anniversary couple. Just provide relevant personal information, and these guys do the work for you.

Commemorative Anniversary Certificate

www.galleryoflove.net 🎁🎁/personalized and unframed

The Together Forever personalized commemorative marriage certificate celebrates the original vows of the golden couple and is customized to celebrate their honored anniversary year. You can order the certificate unframed or in your choice of frames for an additional charge.

Customized Photo Stamps

www.pictureitpostage.com 🎁/sheet of 39¢ stamps

Turn any personal photo into a usable U.S. postage stamp. Transfer the couple's wedding photo to a digital still and upload to the site, select your postage rate, and you'll get a sheet of stamps that you created (one sheet has twenty stamps).

King and Queen Towels

www.kookootowels.com 🎁/each

They warrant the regal titles, no? Two 100 percent cotton terry bath towels are each embroidered with a cute picture and the title "King" or "Queen."

Music of the Year

www.poopsies.com 🎁

Each CD features music from a specified year ranging from 1930 to 1990. Pick their wedding year and bring back the memories.

Message on a Wine Bottle

www.gotgreatgifts.com 🎁/two labels

These Betsybaloo adhesive labels are easy to peel and stick over the existing label on a bottle of wine to create an instant greeting card.

Personalized Photo Frame

www.marye-kelley.com 🎁🎁

These colorful photo frames can customize a favorite photo with a name, monogram, or message under the window. Choose from tons of print styles.

Ball and Chain Mug Set

www.ournameismud.com 🎁🎁

Ceramic painted mug set with one mug that says "Ball" and the other that says "Chain." There is a cute little heart at the bottom of each mug, so no feelings will be hurt.

Glass Cornish Heart

www.simonpearce.com 🎁🎁

This clear glass heart sits on its side and can be engraved with a message for an additional fee.

THE GAY HOORAY

It may be the hardest thing a person does in his or her life: announce to the world that they are gay. There's the fear of rejection, hostility, and worse, not fitting in with their new friends. But for a newly out individual, there's also a certain liberation as they throw open those closet doors and announce, "Yep, I'm gay!" The Gay Hooray embodies that attitude—the exuberant joy and relief in having finally revealed their secret and being able to live the life they want to live. So for these brave individuals, toast to their outing with an outing. Sign them up for an exotic and exclusively all-gay trip, where they can mingle with other interesting folks from their new community. Or make a donation in their honor to a socially conscious organization working to support gays and lesbians. Or for those with a sense of humor, who are more willing to appreciate the lighter side of these major developments, pour on the pop culture and give them a crash course in Gay 101. No matter what you do, be sensitive. How you handle their news will affect them more than you know.

The Advocate Subscription

www.advocate.com 🎁🎁/year

Since 1967, *The Advocate* magazine has been giving the 411 on important news and issues affecting the gay and lesbian community. Articles cover the latest in news, health, the arts, entertainment, and opinion.

Human Rights Campaign Membership

www.hrc.org donations at your own discretion

Give someone a gift of membership to the Human Rights Campaign, and they will receive a year's subscription to HRC's quarterly magazine, along with a *Being Out Rocks* CD—a twenty-one-track CD that benefits the Human Rights Campaign Foundation and features a wide variety of artists including the B-52's, Ani Difranco, Rufus Wainwright, k.d. lang, and Matt Zarley.

Equality Bracelet

http://hrccornerstore.myimagefirst.com/store/ 🎁

The stainless steel Equality Cuff features the Human Rights Campaign Equality logo. The inside is left blank for personalization.

Atlantis Cruise

www.atlantisevents.com 🎁🎁🎁🎁🎁

Hop aboard an all-gay cruise liner. Atlantis Cruises operate first-class cruise ships that are chartered exclusively for gay and lesbian passengers. Luxuries are the same as on an ordinary cruise—excellent food and service, entertainment, activities—you're just among an all-gay passenger list. Destinations cover Central America, South America, Europe, the Caribbean, Alaska, and more.

The Gay 100: A Ranking of the Most Influential Gay Men and Lesbians, Past and Present

www.capricornslair.com 🎁

This 385-page book covers 2,500 years of gay culture and lists profiles of those who have profoundly shaped gay and lesbian culture. One hundred essays shed light on the history of homosexuality.

Membership to Bally Fitness

www.ballyfitness.com 🎁🎁🎁+

Now that they're on the market, it's time to get in shape. Treat them to a gym membership at Bally Fitness, which has over four hundred locations nationwide.

Condomania Pleasure Pack

www.condomania.com 🎁🎁

The Condomania Pleasure Pack contains a selection of unique condoms and lubricants for an exciting experience. There are twenty-seven condoms, ten lube pillows, a detailed full-color guide book, and a few extra goodies.

Now That I'm Out What Do I Do?

www.amazon.com 🎁

Brian McNaught hopes to provide some insight and guidance in this book, where he shares his own experiences in coming out.

Cher Fan Club Membership

www.officialcherfanclub.com 🎁/year

Sign them up for a yearlong membership to the Official Cher Fan Club and they'll receive a fan club welcome letter, exclusive official fan club magnet, autographed photo of

Cher, opportunity to purchase concert tickets to select shows, fan club exclusive contests and giveaways, special exclusive desktop backgrounds, and more.

Sex and the City—The Complete Series (Collector's Gift Set)

www.hbo.com

All six seasons of this hit HBO favorite are assembled in a brilliant collection. The excellent adventures of Carrie, Samantha, Miranda, and Charlotte as they mate, date, and relate in the city.

The L Word Complete First Season

www.sho.com

This provocative and sexy Showtime Network program chronicles the lives of a group of Los Angeles–based friends, some of whom are lesbians, as they navigate careers, families, friendships, personal issues, and romances. Collection contains the series' first fourteen episodes.

"loveisloveislove" T-shirt

www.cafepress.com/glaad

This GLAAD-produced 100 percent cotton girl's-cut baseball jersey says "loveisloveislove" across the chest and "www.glaad.org" at the back of the neck. White shirt comes with sleeves in pink, baby blue, or black.

RSVP Vacation

www.rsvpvacations.com

RSVP Vacations specializes in all-gay and all-lesbian vacation packages. Whether it's a cruise, boat excursion, land tour, or exotic resort, RSVP will have a package to whisk them away on a relaxing trip.

Madonna—The Immaculate Collection DVD

www.amazon.com

Released in 1990, this DVD collection of Madonna's early videos is a classic. Relive the '80s with Madge's groundbreaking videos for "Lucky Star," "Like a Virgin," "Borderline," "Material Girl," "Papa Don't Preach," and more.

The Joy of Gay Sex

www.amazon.com

This is the go-to guide for gay men on all aspects involving gay sex. This 336-page third edition covers safety and health in sex practices of all varieties, emotional issues, relationship arrangements, and ways to meet men. Plus it is newly illustrated.

On Our Backs: Guide to Lesbian Sex

www.amazon.com

World-renowned "sexperts" cover everything from kissing, cruising, and detailed sexual practices to broader conversations on women's sexuality in general.

Celebration Cookies

www.beautifulcookies.com

This tin comes filled with twenty-four gourmet sugar cookies that are decorated as colorful martini glasses and include a special "Cheers!" cookie in the mix. Perfect celebratory and tasty way to offer congratulations on their big news.

Same-Sex-Attracting Cologne

www.pherone.com

Pherone makes specially formulated colognes that are supposed to contain certain pheromones that work their magic on the person you're trying to attract. The Formula G-3 is designed for men to attract other men, and the Formula V-5 is designed for women to attract other women. Each bottle has 5 mg of human pheromones in 10 ml of solution.

Damron City Guide

www.damron.com

Damron publishes five annual printed guidebooks for sophisticated gay and lesbian travelers. The City Guide edition features more than 130 full-color maps pinpointing gay and lesbian accommodations, bars, and bookstores in seventy-five major cities and resort destinations in the United States, Canada, Europe, the Caribbean, South Africa, and Australia. Comprehensive info boxes give you directions from the airport, local hotlines, transit and tourist details.

Rainbow LED Color-Changing Paper Lantern

www.clubthings.com

This paper lantern uses color-changing LEDs to morph through a rainbow of colors. A fun novelty light to have on at a party, it's battery-operated so it can be hung up anywhere without worrying about cords. Lantern is 10" in diameter when assembled.

Pride Silk Bedding

www.rainbow-living.com

This silk quilt has "Pride" written on it in Chinese. Available in mint, lavender, silver, and ivory. Matching pillow shams are available for an additional charge.

Closet Makeover

www.closetsbydesign.com prices vary

Now that they're out of it, how about a closet makeover? Sign them up for an appointment with Closets by Design. With locations in over twenty-five states, Closets by Design will start with a free consultation and then build a customized, organized closet to suit their needs.

Veuve Clicquot Champagne Basket

www.winebasket.com

The Veuve Clicquot congratulations gift features a polished aluminum champagne chiller filled with Veuve Ponsadrin Brut champagne, imported Capelin Black Caviar, zesty gourmet crackers, and "cinnful" coco pecans.

Closet Hanger Sachet

http://store.touchofivy.com

They may not be in it anymore, but they can still keep it smelling fresh. These retro fabric closet sachets have a convenient loop to hang on a hanger to keep clothes nicely scented.

When I Knew

www.amazon.com

This collection of coming-out stories—some touching and some humorous—share the memories of select individuals of when they first realized that they were gay or lesbian.

Gayellow Pages

www.damron.com

This directory of LGBT businesses and resources covers everything in the United States and Canada.

THE MOMMY-ANY-MINUTE

Merriam-Webster's Medical Dictionary defines *pregnant* as "containing unborn young within the body." That's it. There's no mention of suffering from unreasonable food cravings, operating on swollen ankles, maintaining hormonal instability, or juggling frequent trips to the bathroom. If the experience of being pregnant is as simple as "containing unborn young," then why are there so many products and services out there that cater to the well-being of a woman on the verge (of having a baby)? A Mommy-Any-Minute is a woman in need who will appreciate anything to make her feel rested, relaxed, reassured, and lest we forget—ravishing. There are unique prepackaged gift sets filled with comforting products to satisfy everything from the labor of labor to the strain of sleepless nights. There are soft PJs to make her feel sexy in an otherwise drab maternity ward, with the convenient design features she'll need when that baby decides to say hi. And once she gets home, she'll be grateful for the variety of baby organizers, guides, and gadgets to help keep everything in check with her new earthling. Whatever you do, sing her praises, because after nine months of weight gain, waddling, and stretch marks, this mama is the one who deserves to be pampered.

Plush Robe and Slipper Gift Set

www.plushnecessities.com 🎁🎁🎁

Perfect for the hospital or when she gets home, this ultra-cozy gift set includes a Plush Signature Robe and Plush Signature Slippers. Robe arrives boxed in a translucent gift box with a navy blue grosgrain ribbon bow, and slippers are wrapped in a white satin mesh bag. Plush signature items are made of a superfine microfiber material and come in eight gorgeous colors.

Mom Agenda

www.seejanework.com 🎁🎁🎁

She can keep her life straight with this convenient Mom Agenda. It has pages for planning her personal life, but also has separate spaces for the kids' activities. The bound agenda is stylishly made of durable and stain-resistant shantung fabric.

Pregnancy Piercing

www.babiesnbellies.com 🎁

Does she want to keep that belly button piercing but is afraid of her expanding size? These pregnancy piercings can be put in its place for the term of a pregnancy. Made of medical-grade, nonmetallic material, the long, flexible posts allow for plenty of room for skin to move, and she won't have to worry about losing the hole. Stays put with two secure end balls that come in a variety of colors.

"Mommy-to-Be" Sexy Cami Set

www.bellablumaternity.com

This black or white tank and panties set has "mommy-to-be" blazed across the chest in fancy crystals.

New Mom Loungewear

www.bellablumaternity.com

She'll feel pretty in the hospital in the Rebecca lounge set from the Mommy Fabulous collection. This 100 percent white cotton maternity sleeveless top with white silky trim is fully lined and has a side button for easy breast-feeding. The maternity pants have an elasticized waistband and a stylishly flared leg.

A Pregnant Girl's Life Milestone Calendar

www.missfitzinc.com

The pregnancy record calendar/journal comes with stickers to mark all of the important pregnancy events: "Ultrasound," "Baby Shower," "First Kick," "Dr.'s Appointment," and more.

"Not Finding Out" T-shirt

www.dueandsprout.com

This long-sleeve crew neck maternity tee should protect them from having to answer that same clichéd question over and over again.

Baby Briefcase

www.peanutbutterandlili.com

She can keep her new baby's junk organized with a baby briefcase. Lots of pockets for a birth certificate, warranties, insurance forms, thank-yous—name it, and there's a place for it in here. Frosted plastic case comes with file folders in periwinkle, mint, and peach.

Mama Mio Mini Kit

www.mamamio.com

Make sure she stays pampered while preggo! The Mama Mio Mini Kit contains the whole Mama Mio product line in travel-sized containers, including Tummy Rub to de-itch, Boob Tube for bust firming, Wonder-ful Balm for dry patches, Moisturizing Shower Cream, Hydrating Body Cream, and a tiny scented candle.

Mama Mio It's Time! Hospital Kit

www.mamamio.com

Slip this in her suitcase on the way out the door, and once she's at the hospital, she'll appreciate how it warms up her room. Kit includes a Gravida Candle, Calming Facial Spritz, Tummy Rub, and a Mini Massage Oil.

Baby Health Organizer

www.babycenter.com

There's a lot of anxiety in having a baby, and attention to medical details are key. With the Baby Health Organizer, they'll get a refillable binder with tab separators and places to record questions and answers, notes, pockets for storing receipts and doctor's advice, customizable blank folders, and more.

Happy Parent Kit

www.kookootowels.com 🎁🎁

Gift set that comes with 100 percent cotton seersucker PJ bottoms and a matching terry hand towel, both embroidered with either "new mom," "mom to be," or "new dad."

First Sounds Recording System

www.pampermematerinity.com 🎁🎁

With the First Sounds Recording System, a soon-to-be mom can listen to the sounds that are going on inside her belly. The system includes a set of headphones attached to a device that lets you listen to and record the sounds of an unborn baby.

"Just Delivered" Tank Top

www.dueandsprout.com 🎁🎁

In case they were wondering, this simple black tank with "Just Delivered" in blue on the chest does the talking for her.

Racy Red Nursing Bra

www.evalillian.com 🎁🎁

This sexy bright red nursing bra by Eve Alexander gives new meaning to "Oh, Mama!" Design is a romantic red with a floral lace pattern with adjustable straps and a soft, unlined cup. Comes with a matching adjustable bikini panty for an extra $12.99.

Pregnancy Henna Kit

www.doulashop.com 🎁

There's a tradition to have a henna ceremony on the mom-to-be's belly as the delivery date nears in order to protect the mom and baby with good spirits during labor. It's also an opportunity for the mom to relax and have a spiritual moment with her child. Among the items included in the kit are henna powder, essential oils, applicator accessories, recipes, and instructions. Check with a doctor before using a henna kit.

Boppy Cuddle Pillow

www.lullabylane.com 🎁🎁

The Boppy Cuddle Pillow is perfect for when it's time for her to sleep on her side. This uniquely shaped pillow supports the belly and helps to keep the back aligned properly. The washable slipcover is made from 320-count cotton.

Girlfriend's Guide to Baby Gear

http://us.penguingroup.com 🎁

She may be about to be a mom, but she's always a consumer first. This guide gives the 411 on when to skimp and when to splurge; how to pick safe hand-me-downs; do's and don'ts for crib and car seats, plus more.

Belly Bars

www.babycenter.com 🎁🎁/twelve-pack

Stamped with approval by an ob-gyn, Nutrabella's Belly Bars are delicious and nutritional and provide her with key prenatal vitamins and minerals needed preconception, during pregnancy, and while nursing. Flavor choices are Berry Nutty Cravings, Mellow Oat, and Baby Needs Chocolate.

Sexy Maternity Lingerie

www.tippeetoes.com 🎁🎁

Do whatever you can to bring it on. This white silk and lace babydoll nightie is a special treat for a mom-to-be.

Postpartum Recovery Kit

www.earthmamaangelbaby.com

Earth Mama Angel Baby realizes a woman's body was just sent through the ringer to get that kid out into the world. The Recovery Kit comes with a variety of special organic products to help ease the postdelivery pains, including Postpartum Recovery Tea, Postpartum Recovery Bath Herbs, New Mama Bottom Spray, Happy Mama Spray, and Earth Mama Bottom Balm.

Labor Ease Kit

www.earthmamaangelbaby.com

Comfort is key when you're squeezing out a child. The Earth Mama Angel Baby Labor Ease Kit comes with organic products to help relieve the anguish of labor, including Labor Ease Massage Oil, a lullaby CD, Labor Ease Tea, Mint Herbal Lip Balm, and a Hot Spot Labor Sock.

Eternal Maternal Belly Cast Kit

www.tippeetoes.com

OK, so she may feel like she never wants to be this big again . . . but she'll thank you later for the plaster belly cast of her bump. The Belly Cast Kit comes with a plastic dropcloth, rolls of plaster gauze, Eternal Maternal belly lube, three feet of picture wire, hook and nail, and of course, instruction on how she's supposed to do this!

The Baby Bistro Box

www.babybistrobrands.com

The Baby Bistro Box makes it easy to figure out what foods are good for a new babe. It's filled with nutritional guidance, baby food recipes, and grocery tips. The box is color-coded to cover every stage of a baby's life through his or her entire first year.

52 Tips for New Parents Cards

www.bestbabyshower.com 🎁

This deck of cards featuring fifty-two practical tips will help new parents adjust with suggestions for ways to reduce isolation, calm a screamer, maintain a social life, and more.

Mommy-Time Essentials Kit

www.tuttibella.com 🎁🎁

Hospital robes are so drab. This Mommy-Time Essentials Kit comes with some more feminine options for hospital style. It comes with a cozy pink cotton nursing gown, lush socks with slip-proof bottoms, and a headband to keep her hair in check.

Mommy-to-Be Hipster Panty

www.unbuttonedmaternity.com 🎁

For the expectant mom, she can feel secretly sexy with these comfortable white hipster panties with "mommy-to-be" printed in rhinestones across the front.

Mommy-to-Be Pregnancy Gift Set

www.nybeautysecrets.com 🎁🎁

Erbaviva's Mommy-to-Be Pregnancy Gift Set is made up of soothing milk powder blended with essential oils of lavender, lemon, and sandalwood to relax and moisturize. The set also includes a Stretch Mark Oil and a Back Rub Oil and the three are packaged in a natural fiber gift bag with a satin bow.

Glamourmom Nursing Tank Top

www.tinytots.com 🎁🎁

The Glamourmom Nursing Bra Tank manages to provide postpartum tummy coverage with a built-in soft cup frame and elastic shelf for total breast support. A light mesh liner holds nursing pads in place when opening flaps.

Gourmet Premade Meal

www.alazing.com 🎁+

There will be no time for cooking as soon as she gets home, so treat her (and her honey) to a prepared gourmet meal delivered straight to her door.

Gorgeous Beatrix Potter Cookies

www.beautifulcookies.com 🎁🎁

Inspired by Beatrix Potter, this gift tin holds sixteen gourmet sugar cookies, each adorned with the storybook images of Peter Rabbit, Benjamin Bunny, Tom Kitten, and Jemima Puddle Duck.

Session with a Massage Doula

www.massagedoula.com prices vary

Massage Doulas are certified massage therapists who have completed advanced certification in prenatal massage, postpartum massage, labor, delivery support, and infant massage. If you go to this site, you can find a certified massage doula in the mom-to-be's city. Prices will vary. If you don't find one where she lives, many spas will offer special pregnancy massages.

Pregnancy Mug

www.bestbabyshower.com 🎁

This hilarious ten-ounce ceramic mug is shaped like the torso of a very pregnant woman.

Luxe Leather Brag Book

www.katespade.com 🎁🎁🎁

They're going to ask to see pictures, so now she can carry her new baby's mug around in an elegant leather brag book. The Kate Spade Jane Street Elyce Brag Book has soft calfskin lining, tab closure, and comes in three different colors.

Mother and Baby Spa Basket

www.sabonnyc.com 🎁🎁

Packaged in an elegant Sabon Box are Mother & Baby Body Oil, Mother & Baby Lotion, and soap on a rope.

Nursing Cover

www.bebeaulait.com 🎁🎁

Nursing cover-up for moms . . . stylish, and maintains modesty!

Once She's Home

www.babybox.com 🎁🎁

Give her Momease—The New Mother Comfort Kit because she deserves a little attention too . . . an elegant tote bag packed with aromatherapy bath and body products, a journal, and a tranquil CD.

Dad Duties

www.diaperdudebag.com 🎁🎁

This unassuming diaper bag is for the dad who wants to keep his cool. Looks like a camouflage messenger bag but comes equipped with all the necessary pockets.

Caring for Your Baby and Young Child, Revised Edition: Birth to Age 5

www.amazon.com 🎁

Produced by the American Academy of Pediatrics, this 784-page hefty bible is a comprehensive parenting manual, and includes a month-by-month guide to the first year, nutritional information, basic care instructions, and physical, emotional, and social developmental milestones for children up to five.

Complete Idiot's Guide to Fatherhood

http://us.penguingroup.com 🎁

He'd better be ready by now, but just in case . . . this book will save him when he's in trouble.

New Parent Apology Cards

www.bestbabyshower.com 🎁

These cheeky apology cards are convenient to hand out whenever their baby becomes someone else's problem. Set comes with two each of fifteen different apologies.

New Mommy Make a Wish Necklace

www.unbuttonedmaternity.com 🎁

Created by Dogeared, this little sterling wishbone is ¼" on a peridot silk string with sterling clasp. Mom is to put the necklace on and make a wish for her and her new baby and as soon as it wears off, the wish will come true.

Belly Doodles

www.bestbabyshower.com

It's sticking out, so why not decorate! This set of ten belly tattoos comes with different sayings, including "This Belly Rocks," "Will Kick for Ice Cream," and "Under Construction."

THE STAR MITZVAH

In cultures around the world, traditional rites of passage mark the moment a child becomes an adult. For Jews, this sacred event is called a Bar (if you're a boy) or a Bat (if you're a girl) Mitzvah and usually happens around the age of thirteen, when it's thought a child is old enough to accept the responsibilities of adulthood. To celebrate this occasion, the Star Mitzvah reluctantly agrees to become the center of attention for an entire weekend, awkwardly reciting prayers before hundreds of giggling friends, beaming relatives, and total strangers. Then mazel tov! They're instant grown-ups.

Reality check: At age thirteen, most boys still dress in clothes their mothers bought them and sing like Peter Brady on a good day. Most girls are just graduating from training bras and are desperately trying to nail the perfect eyeliner-to-eye-shadow ratio. Adults? Hardly. But for their efforts, they are feted with a killer party and plenty of presents. For gifts, you've got two choices. You can either bestow relevant Judaic items: an ornate tallit (prayer shawl), a personal wine cup, or meaningful Jewish literature. Or you can shower them with anything a typical pubescent kid would have on a wish list: iPods, makeup, or cold hard cash. Either way, after a weekend overload of pinched cheeks, juicy kisses, and congratulatory hugs, what this "adult" may really need is a drink.

Mini-Torah

www.jillery.com 🎁🎁🎁

Decorated clear lucite Torah stand stands only 9¼" high and contains an actual mini-Torah scroll.

Gold Name Necklace

www.zionjudaica.com 🎁🎁

This 14k gold necklace is personalized to feature a Bat Mitzvah's name in English or Hebrew. Her name hangs from a 16" chain.

Shofar

www.keterjudaica.com 🎁+

A shofar (a ram's horn) is blown on the holiest days of the Jewish year—Rosh Hashana and Yom Kippur. It's usually a favorite part of the service.

Tallit Set

www.zionjudaica.com 🎁🎁+

As he becomes an adult, a gift of his first tallit will be a keepsake he will hold onto for the rest of his life. Choose from a wide assortment of tallit styles and colors. Each set comes with a coordinated tallit bag.

Velvet Tallit Bag

www.a-zara.com

Or if he already has a tallit, a velvet tallit bag will keep it safe and clean. The bag measures 11.25" × 14", has a zipper close, and comes in midnight blue, dark blue, and dark burgundy. Bag can be personalized for an additional charge.

Elsa Peretti Star of David Necklace

www.tiffany.com

As she becomes a woman, shouldn't she be introduced to Tiffany? This platinum Star of David pendant hangs from a 16" chain and is an Elsa Peretti design.

Custom Bar Mitzvah Cuff Links

www.judaicaworldwide.com

Sterling silver cuff links have a background of Jerusalem's Western Wall and are personalized with the Bar Mitzvah boy's Hebrew name in 14k gold.

Bar/Bat Mitzvah Lithograph

www.judaicaworldwide.com

The name and date of the Bar/Bat Mitzvah is done in hand calligraphy in both English and Hebrew and arches over the Haftorah portion of the appropriate week. Approx. 18" × 19".

Nambé Kiddush Cup

www.nambe.com

This simple, sleek, and elegant Kiddush Cup (wine cup) by Nambé is made of metal and stainless steel and is 7" high.

TANAKH: The Holy Scriptures: Presentation Edition

www.jewishpub.org

The JPS *TANAKH* edition of the Holy Scriptures is widely regarded as the standard English translation throughout the English-speaking world. It is the culmination of three decades of collaboration by academic scholars and rabbis, representing the three largest branches of organized Judaism in the United States. A presentation box holds the black leatherette-bound 1,622-page book.

A Historical Atlas of the Jewish People

www.judaicawebstore.com

This hardcover book details the story of the Jewish people from the time of the patriarchs to the present. This comprehensive tome uses illustrations, maps, photography, and commentary to take us through history. It's edited by Eli Barnavi, the director of the Department of History at the University of Tel Aviv and associate professor at the École des Haute Études et Sciences Sociales in Paris.

But He Was Good to His Mother: The Life and Times of Jewish Gangsters

www.amazon.com

From Benjamin "Bugsy" Siegel to Arthur "Dutch Schultz" Flegenheimer, *But He Was Good to His Mother* tells the stories of old-time Jewish gangsters and how they led a life of crime while maintaining their Jewish roots.

Jewish Women Speak about Jewish Matters

www.amazon.com

This book sheds some light on the Jewish woman's point of view through a collection of essays by female teachers of

Jewish ideas around the world. It covers subjects including gender issues, relationships, marriage, beauty, Shabbat, prayer, work, and more.

Jewish Women in America: An Historical Encyclopedia
www.barnesandnoble.com 🎁🎁🎁🎁
This voluminous biographical encyclopedia introduces over eight hundred diverse Jewish women in America dating back to 1654, when the first Jewish woman arrived here. Each entry is comprised of a biography and an essay about that person.

Tallit Clips
www.judaicawebstore.com 🎁🎁
Keep it together with these sterling Hazorfim tallit clips.

Israeli Hip-Hop
www.judaicawebstore.com 🎁
Yes, hip-hop is universal. *Subliminal: The Light and the Shadow* is a CD full of Hebrew hip-hop from one of the leading groups in Israel.

Flip-Top Note Cards
www.galison.com 🎁
These adorable stationery sets by Galison come with twelve notecards and thirteen color-coordinated envelopes, all housed in a hard flip-top box. Sets are available in twelve cute designs.

Sterling Silver Candlesticks
www.silversnobs.com 🎁🎁🎁🎁
Every Friday night, candles are lit to mark the beginning of

the Sabbath. A personal set of 4¼" candlesticks by Empire Silver will make this tradition more personal.

Tzedakah Box

www.judaica-mall.com 🎁🎁

It's just like a piggy bank, but when full, all the contents go to charity. This square wooden box is painted with images of the colorful scenes of Jerusalem.

Plant a Tree in Israel

www.jnf.org 🎁

It's been a long-standing tradition to celebrate a person by planting a tree in Israel in their honor. Through the Jewish National Fund, you can plant a tree and select a theme for dedication.

Personalized Bat Mitzvah Photo Frame

www.jennibick.com 🎁🎁 (personalized 5 × 7)

Jenni Bick is on Oprah's favorites list, and she's designed a photo frame especially for Bar and Bat Mitzvah kids. Each paper frame features a collage with Hebrew calligraphy and beads as an accent to represent a torah scroll. The frames can be customized with the celebrant's name and the date of the Bar/Bat Mitzvah.

Xperience Choice

www.xperiencedays.com 🎁🎁🎁+

Whether you think they'll like surfing the ocean, free-falling from the sky, or getting pampered at a luxury spa, there is a guaranteed winning experience waiting for them to enjoy. With Xperience Choice, the adventure is on you, but you leave the selection up to them. Certificates start at

$100 and go up to $125,000 (but that would be one lucky kid!).

Chai Dollars

It's a Jewish tradition to give money in multiples of eighteen. In the Hebrew alphabet, each letter corresponds to a number, and the two letters that form the word *chai* (Hebrew for "life") add up to eighteen. So, traditionally, you give a Bar or Bat Mitzvah $18 or $36 or $72, and so on. You can either give this in cash or as a gift certificate to a favorite store like Sharper Image or Sephora.

Men's Heavy Sterling Silver ID Bracelet

www.100silver.com 🎁🎁🎁

An ID bracelet is a manly way to dress up an otherwise ordinary look.

Harvey Nagila Dancing Doll

www.traditionsjewishgifts.com 🎁

This funny sound/touch-activated novelty doll dances to the song "Hava Nagila." Batteries are included.

Sephora

www.sephora.com 🎁+

A gift card to a Sephora store is like letting a kid loose in a candy store. There is everything here for girls and guys from perfume and cologne to hair products to soaps and lip glosses. The Sephora gift card comes in a sleek, black, dual-mirrored compact embossed with the Sephora logo. Available in denominations of $25 to $250.

Bar/Bat Mitzvah Memory Album Box

www.lexingtonstudios.com

The Mitzvah box is a full album with standard 8.5" × 11" sheet protectors and acid-free paper. Attached to the bottom of the album is a 2"-deep box to put additional mementos and keepsakes, or even all the cards received at the event. The entire thing is made of wood with brass hinges and posts. It can be personalized with the actual invitation for an additional fee.

Personalized Menorah

www.jillery.com

Rounded, tempered glass, 5.5" × 9" menorah with steel candle holders and an etched Star of David design. Personalized name is added under the top arc.

iPod Video

http://store.apple.com

With amazing clarity in digital audio and video, the iPod Video is everyone's favorite gift. They can download any music, audiobooks, podcasts, or video streams available to the iPod family.

THE LAID UP AND LONELY

You know how crappy it feels to be sick. Your breath stinks, your body throbs, and no one wants to come near you. Whether you're home with the flu or in a hospital attached to an IV, being sick sucks. So, the Laid Up and Lonely are left to suffer in solitude and yearn for the days when they can once again mingle with the masses. In the meantime, they're going to need some serious TLC. They crave gadgets and distractions that keep them entertained while awake and make their new bed-bound berth a little more bearable. If they're able to roam, they'll want to relieve their achy muscles with comforting bath bits designed to soak them into shape and leave them feeling fresh. And once their appetite returns, you can help them transition to solid foods with goodies that welcome them back to health. When it comes to spoiling the unwell, it's an easy win; they'll appreciate any sign of life from the outside world . . . as long as no shots are required.

Colorful Notebook

www.carrotandstickpress.com

While they're stuck in bed, they can start a journal to log their day-to-day health news. Plus these are just really gorgeous notebooks! Covers come in eighteen different styles; 5.5" × 8", sixty-four blank pages.

Suede Slippers

www.lisab.com

Luxury suede slippers come in a slew of colors for men and women.

Bored Games Basket

www.gothambaskets.com

Gotham Baskets presents the Bored Games Basket for that person who's bed bound. Basket comes with mini pool table game, five-minute mysteries, fine art puzzle, conundrum puzzle book, get well fortune cookies, chocolate Band-Aids, wishing you a sweet recovery lemon drops, metal puzzles, world's largest crossword or word search, six-in-one game set (chess/checkers/backgammon/cribbage/dominoes/cards), mystery game jigsaw puzzle, and aquabotics (water mazes).

Comfortable Pajamas

www.thepajamastore.com

Choose from dozens of pajama styles for women from designers like Bedhead, the Cat's Pajamas, Tepper Jackson, and more. Men's prep school–style pajamas are also available for the guys.

Barefoot Dreams Cozy Chic Throw

www.nordstrom.com 🎁🎁🎁

This cushy 54" × 72" throw blanket will keep them comfortable in bed. It's made of a luxuriously soft fabric and is available in camel, espresso, pink, sea glass, cream, and taupe.

Levenger Large Laplander

www.levenger.com 🎁🎁

This lap desk makes it easy and comfortable to turn a bed into a desk. The smooth, hard top is a maple and cherry veneer in both a light or natural shade, and sits on top of a soft neoprene cushion. Desk top also has two elastic cloth straps to keep papers and pens in place.

New York Times *Tough Crosswords Vol. 13*

www.nytstore.com 🎁

One hundred of the most challenging puzzles from the pages of the *New York Times.*

Books on Tape

www.simplyaudiobooks.com 🎁+

If reading is too much of a strain, get them some books on tape/CD. All they have to do is hit Play, and the story comes to them. It's a good way to stay preoccupied and busy. Simply Audiobooks offers more than 18,000 titles for purchase. They will gift wrap and send directly to the sicko's door.

Bright Silk Pillowcases

www.uncommonscents.com 🎁🎁

They're bright and silky and make being stuck in bed not so

bad. The DreamSacks Charmeuse Silk pillowcases come with two standard-sized cases in an array of colors.

Bedside Carafe

www.cb2.com

This modernist glass water carafe has simple lines, and the carafe lid doubles as a drinking glass. Nicely styled for bedside use.

Pathlighter Lighted Cane

www.vitalitymedical.com

It's a cane . . . it's a night-light. This aluminum and polycarbonate cane is the standard 36" high and features a light-up shaft so they can see as they hobble around in the dark.

Seda France "Get Well" Candle

www.sedafrance.com

Seda France's L'Occasion line of candles send a message along with a great scent. Their "Get Well" candle smells like sage and comes in their signature yellow box with a satin ribbon tied around it that says "Get Well" in both English and French. Candle burns for forty hours.

Grandma's Chicken Soup

www.grandmaschickensoup.com

The Grandma's Chicken Soup Get Well Basket comes with one half-gallon portion of Grandma's chicken soup (can add matzo balls or noodles if you want), as well as a giant ceramic mug and matching spoon, a mini *Chicken Soup for the Soul* book, a package of "Get Well Soon" shaped pasta and other treats, and Grandma's signature Carrot Pen.

The Superior Comfort Bed Lounger

www.hammacher.com

This fully adjustable lounger will make the confines of the bedroom a little more comfortable. The adjustable headrest automatically follows their head's movements, the arms swing into their body for support, and a lumbar pillow can be adjusted to give maximum back support. There are even pockets for a remote and reading material.

Tonsillectomy Survival Kit

www.icecreamsource.com

Thoughtful and relieving, the Tonsillectomy Survival Kit sends the bed-bound a case of Popsicles containing orange, grape, and cherry Popsicles, Creamsicle pops, and Fudgsicle pops.

Spa Soak

www.aromafloria.com

Achy muscles get a break with the Aromafloria Stress Less Spa at Home Kit. It comes with muscle soak lotion, mineral salts, bath and body massage oil, a soy lite travel candle, and a wooden massager.

Nosey Cups

www.medsupplyco.com

These plastic cups are designed so they can easily drink without having to lift their head; there's a convenient cutout for a nose. Set comes with three Nosey Cups in varying sizes.

Yoga in Bed Book

www.bordersstores.com

Keep them active with some healthy stretching and yoga poses. This book walks even a beginner through easy and relaxing yoga movement that can be done from the comfort of a bed.

Shiatsu Massage Bed Rest with LED Reading Light

www.sharperimage.com

Read in bed and get a shiatsu massage! This ergonomically designed bed rest is made of soft faux-suede upholstery and features built-in Shiatsu-style kneading massage nodes, a built-in LED reading light, a cup holder, and a large side pocket.

XM Portable Satellite Radio

www.xmradio.com

The Delphi XM MyFi Satellite Radio system will allow them to listen to XM channels live coast to coast by satellite in bed. Once they're out of bed, the included car kit and home kit will come in handy.

Electronic Handheld Sudoku

www.amazon.com

This handheld Sudoku game features one million puzzles, five levels of difficulty, memory, and a timer.

"Get Well Soon" Cookie Cake

www.mrsfields.com

Mrs. Fields makes a 12" cookie cake decorated on top with "Get Well Soon." Cake comes in five different cookie flavors.

Personal Percussion Massager with Heat

www.sharperimage.com 🎁🎁

This lightweight handheld massager uses gel nodes to provide a deep muscle massage. Also has an option to turn on the heat.

3-D Puzzles

www.areyougame.com 🎁+

They may want to wait until they're out of bed to try these. These 3-D jigsaw puzzles add another dimension of difficulty to jigsaws. Choose from dozens of locations to re-create, including Notre Dame, the Capitol, a medieval castle, or even all of New York City (3,141 pieces).

Paint-by-Number Kit

www.chroniclebooks.com 🎁

Create your own masterpiece from bed. This complete kit comes with eight paint-by-numbers postcards, eight stick-back easels, twelve different acrylic paints, a paintbrush, and how-to book.

American College of Physicians Complete Home Medical Guide

www.amazon.com 🎁🎁

In this thick tome, you'll find information on causes, symptoms, diagnoses, treatments, and prevention of medical conditions, plus over 2,000 illustrations.

Spade Playing Cards

www.umbra.com 🎁

A single deck of cards comes in a walnut holder with magnetic closure. Good for solitaire.

THE NOUVEAU DIVORCÉ

Tammy Wynette summed it up when she sang, ". . . this will be pure H-E-double-L for me. Oh, I wish that we could stop this D-I-V-O-R-C-E." A divorce is never easy, even if they're grateful to get rid of the soulless loser. But since nearly 50 percent of marriages end in divorce, the Nouveau Divorcé shouldn't feel singled out. Instead, he or she should feel like one of the gang. Which is why if your suddenly single friend is a blubbering wreck with a bleak outlook on love, convince them to give up the grief and feast on their freedom. Toast to some much-deserved happiness with martinis served up on feisty and inspirational cocktail napkins. Help them reclaim their independence with souvenirs that celebrate the unattached, and send the past packing. And prep them for reentry to the dating world with helpful novelties to get their groove back: whether it's sexy personal pick-me-ups or handy items that will bring them more pleasure in one night than the entire last year of their marriage. The important thing is to celebrate their emancipation, then toss them back to mingle with the other fish in the sea.

"Boyfriend" Arm Pillow

www.whatonearthcatalog.com 🎁

She'll never have to curl up on the couch alone again. This 26" × 27", snuggly, comforting arm will wrap around her and keep her company. Polyester filled with foam.

"Girlfriend" Pillow

www.spilsbury.com 🎁🎁

And he'll never have to be alone again either. This 23"× 13"× 13" pillow shaped like a woman's warm lap is perfect for him to lay his head on and fall asleep. Bonus: it comes dressed in a hot red miniskirt.

Man-Bashing Punching Bag

www.wishingfish.com 🎁

She may need to release some anger with this inflatable punching bag printed with a generic male likeness on front and back. The bottom of the bag is weighted so he won't be sent flying. Punching bag measures approximately 5'.

Voodoo Doll Man

www.plumparty.com 🎁

With this little Voodoo Doll Man, she can inflict a variety of ailments from bladder trouble to sexual malfunction to sagging jowls with a simple prick of a pin. Doll measures 8.5" tall. Pin included.

Complimentary Cereal Bowl

www.ournameismud.com 🎁

Pump up their confidence with some daily affirmation with these 32-oz. ceramic cereal bowls for men and women. For women, the You're a Goddess bowl reads, "You're beautiful! You're amazing! You're Brilliant! Everyone loves you! You're a Goddess!" Or for the men, the Chicks Dig You! bowl reads, "You're the Man! You're Handsome! You're Strong! You're Charming!" Each piece is individually hand-painted, lead-free, dishwasher and microwave safe.

Bottle of Wine Glass

www.lighterside.com

This wineglass will hold an entire bottle of wine. Cheers!

"Big Hug" Mug

www.ournameismud.com

Loving ceramic mug with "Big Hug" painted on it. In red or white.

"I'm In Single Hell" Wineglass

www.eye4gifts.com

The Single Hell ten-ounce wineglass features a hand-painted grumpy looking lady who's holding a martini in one hand and the personals page in the other. She has a classic "Hello" name tag on her basic black dress. "I'm in single hell!!!!" is painted on her base.

"Happiness" Kanji Ornament

www.isabellacatalog.com

Kanji is an ancient Japanese language based on ideograms, with each character having a unique definition. This metal-framed glass ornament features the Kanji symbol for "Happiness."

Sexy Magazine

www.playboy.com or www.playgirl.com 🎁/year

Get them back in the mood with some good old-fashioned nudies! A subscription to *Playgirl* or *Playboy* should do the trick . . . or at least make them giggle once a month.

Survivor's Bracelet

www.ironaccents.com 🎁🎁

This sterling silver bracelet comes with an inspiring note that says: "When the storms of life batter our spirit, with no safe harbor in sight, hold onto the faith deep within you, for it will guide you to safer shores."

"Turn Me On" Remote Control Vibrating Panties

www.bootyparlor.com 🎁🎁🎁

The lace and satin side-tie bikini is outfitted with a vibrating seven-function "bullet" powered entirely by remote control that works from up to twenty feet away. In black or pink.

Subscription to an Online Dating Service

www.match.com 🎁🎁

Make the dive back in to find a new fish on Match.com. Sign them up for however many months you deem appropriate at this proven online dating service.

Playboy Coasters

www.homewetbar.com 🎁

The classic Rabbit Head leather coasters are a must-have for any bachelor. This set of four Playboy coasters is constructed of high-quality die-cast chrome-plated metal with black leather tops and cork bottoms.

Motivational Cocktail Napkins

www.thehappywoman.com

This set of cocktail napkins says "Sin now, pay later." Throw in a bottle of booze to seal the deal.

New Sheets

www.macys.com

The bed is probably the most sensitive place after a breakup, so start fresh with new luxury sheets. Get them the best you can afford; shoot for a 600-thread-count, deliciously soft bedding set and let them sleep in peace.

Hang Gliding Gift

www.signaturedays.com

Send someone off soaring into a new start with a tandem hang gliding session.

Protect This Woman Bracelet

www.femailcreations.com

This sterling silver and 18k gold cuff bracelet was designed to symbolize strength and security. It's hand stamped "Protect this woman" on the inside, and peppered with blue topaz, garnets, amethyst, and peridot stones on the outside.

Bachelor Mop Slippers

www.wishingfish.com

Cleaning is a breeze with these mini-mops/slippers. No bending or lifting needed; just toss them in the wash after a good shuffle.

Tanqueray Martini Gift Basket

www.sendliquor.com 🎁🎁🎁

This Tanqueray Gift Basket comes with all the ingredients for a world-class martini: Tanqueray gin, vermouth, and lots of snacks.

Butt/Face Soap

www.spilsbury.com 🎁

If they're simplifying their life, it doesn't get more basic than this. One bar of soap for use on your face and a separate bar for use on your butt!

Chicken Potpie

www.deandeluca.com 🎁🎁

For the newly single manly man, he just pops this Dean & Deluca Chicken Pot Pie in the oven, and he's got a delicious gourmet meal. Eight inches in diameter.

The Between Boyfriends Book

www.barnesandnoble.com 🎁

From *Sex and the City* scribe Cindy Chupack, this collection of essays covers what women think and deal with when facing the dating world, breakups, and the male species in general.

Break-Up Kit

www.bootyparlor.com 🎁🎁🎁

If you don't, nobody will. This self-affirming love kit comes with assorted goodies, including I'm So Sexy Lipgloss, Dust Up Kissable Body Shimmer, Break-Up Kit booklet, Va-va-voom pink feather boa, totally hot temporary tattoos, and of course, a sex toy, too.

Complete Idiot's Guide to Cooking—For Guys

http://us.penguingroup.com 🎁

Hop to it, mister; you've got no one to cook for you anymore, so the time has come for you to figure out how to whip up some tasty dishes for yourself in the kitchen. More than 230 recipes geared to a guy's healthy appetite.

Get Fresh Look Better Naked Full Body Treatment

www.nybeautysecrets.com 🎁🎁

Now that she's back on the market, better get that skin back to shape. The Look Better Naked set is an all-over body treatment that comes with Lemongrass Salt Scrub, Soy Body Facial, and Lemongrass Body Butter. All three work to exfoliate, detoxify, and refresh depressed skin.

Kabbalah Candle

www.home101store.com 🎁

Slatkin & Co.'s Kabbalah Collection of candles offers up the Spiritual Cleansing candle. The scent is a mix of heliotrope, vanilla, musk, sandalwood, and frangipani and has a burn time of forty-five hours. Each candle comes in a lush red tin to symbolize red's power and energy and is accompanied by a blessed Kabbalah red bracelet to ward off evil.

Breath Palette Zen Palette Toothpaste Kit

www.beautyexclusive.com 🎁

You never know what might work; the secret could be in your toothpaste. Breath Palette has a series of toothpaste kits, including the Zen Palette that contains five small tubes of paste flavored like cola, honey, lavender, lemon tea, and rose.

Nickel Morning After Rescue Gel

www.beautyexclusive.com 🎁🎁

After a tough night out on the town, their face will take a beating from the cigarette smoke, booze, and general party pollution. Nickel's Morning After Rescue Gel should help get their face back to fine form. It contains natural wheat and soybean–based proteins, Hamamelidacea Extract, caffeine, and menthol-enriched unroasted coffee complex to depuff, firm, and stimulate the skin.

Wonder Woman Action Figure

www.toyrocket.com 🎁

She's only five inches tall, but she's still a wonder. This inspiring Wonder Woman action figure comes packaged with a lasso and throwing action.

Celebrity Substitutes

www.hollywoodmegastore.com 🎁🎁

Close enough to the real thing . . . bring a touch of romance to your female friend's life with a realistic cardboard standup of a half-naked Fabio. He stands 6'2" and is ready to be her man. Or for him, Angelina Jolie as Laura Croft is smokin' at 5'9".

Sin City

www.vegas.com prices vary

When you're back to being a bachelor or bachelorette, it's time for a spin to Las Vegas. There are lots of different packages at a range of hotels. Some will include tickets to a show or a dinner.

"All About Me" Crystal Compact

www.shoploveme.com 🎁🎁🎁

Every time she looks in the mirror, she'll have a sparkly reminder of what's most important . . . her! Mirror compact comes bedazzled in Swarovski crystals in your choice of colors.

Heart Towel

www.kookootowels.com 🎁

A big fluffy 100 percent cotton terry towel has a bright red heart embroidered on it so your pal can wrap up in love.

1,001 Meditations by Mike George

www.aromafloria.com 🎁

They can learn to relax and feel centered by reading this book. It recommends inspirational meditations, affirmations, and quotes.

Rugged Leather Journal

www.rusticoleather.com 🎁🎁

The Good Book leather journal has 160 hand-torn pages that are sewn in and closes with a buckle tab. Paper size is 5" × 6.5".

Moan-eek the Maid

www.aboyd.com 🎁🎁🎁🎁

Is he feeling a little lonely around the house? Have Moan-eek the Maid move in. She's a life-size, self-standing doll that will liven things up. She's pretty, quiet, and not wearing very much.

"Change Is Good" Votive

www.ournameismud.com 🎁

This dainty ceramic candle votive has the saying "Change is Good" hand painted around the rim.

Couture Condoms

www.justincaseinc.com 🎁🎁

Be responsible and trendy! These convenient and chic Rendez-Vous Red condom cases look like little compacts and can stylishly be dropped into a purse for a big night out. Compacts are coated in sparkling clear acrylic and open to reveal a mirror. Comes with a red organza gift bag and two Just in Case condoms. The compact is 2½" × 2½".

KISS Kondoms

www.condomania.com 🎁/dozen

KISS Kondoms are the officially licensed condoms of the legendary rock band KISS. The "Tongue Lubricated" Kondoms featuring Gene Simmons are red latex condoms with special "tongue" lubrication.

The Overnighter Kit

www.goodvibes.com 🎁

Just in case she doesn't make it home some nights, this overnight survival kit will keep her happy and safe. It contains: two ounces of Body Oil, one ounce strawberry champagne Body Candy, one ounce Good Lubrications Cream, a rosemary mint candle, two GV Premium Latex Condoms, and a vanilla Pleasure Wipe. The whole set is small enough to fit in a purse.

Devine Toy Box

www.goodvibes.com 🎁🎁

Keep a secret stash of sex toys in this handsome (and locked!) 9" × 4" × 4" faux-leather storage box. The exterior is black and red; the interior satin; the privacy quotient guaranteed with a lock and key.

Sex and the City: Essentials DVD Set

www.hbo.com 🎁🎁

The adventures of Carrie, Samantha, Miranda, and Charlotte continue with this best of set containing four discs: *The Best of Breakups*, *The Best of Lust*, *The Best of Romance*, and *The Best of Mr. Big*.

Mr. Right

www.seejanework.com 🎁

He's a stand-up guy who comes with eight magnetic voice balloons saying all the right things, including these gems: "May I take you shoe shopping?" and "As always, you're right." There are five preprinted magnets and three blank ones so you can fill in whatever it is you want to hear. Measures 3" × 3½" boxed.

I'm Fine! A Really Helpful Guide to the First 100 Days After Your Breakup

www.thehappywoman.com 🎁

No dwelling allowed. *I'm Fine* provides sound advice and remedies for surviving the first one hundred days after the end of a relationship. Look for tips on eluding exes, retail therapy, pampering, and much more.

Tequila Server

www.zippergifts.com 🎁🎁🎁

Celebrate with this sleek all-in-one stainless steel tequila server. It has a shot glass, salt shaker, and spot for a piece of lime.

"Celebrity" Blow-Up Dolls

www.greatpleasures.com 🎁

Now that he's single, how about setting him up with a "celebrity" for a night? These fantasy dolls are probably as close as he'll get to the real thing. Choose from Paris Love Doll, Dirty Christina Doll, JHo Love Doll, or Pamela Doll.

Little Black Book

www.smythson.com 🎁🎁

Folks, that's what it's here for. This high-end black lambskin address book has silver-edged paper and "Little Black Book" stamped in silver on the front.

THE HOUSEWARMEE

Moving into a new home is a time of excitement, anticipation, and the satisfaction of a job well done. It's also a time of debt, anxiety, and fatigue. As soon as moving boxes arrive, the new home owner begins the arduous task of uncovering which precious items lost their lives in limbo. Eventually, the dust settles and the Housewarmee can put down the paintbrush to emerge master of this new domain. Once their doors are open, you can find plenty of unique housewarming gifts that will bring special finishing touches to a new casa. Traditional gifts are a good housebreaker and always unexpected; giving a pineapple or salt and bread are age-old symbols of hospitality. Monogrammed linens or serving items help bring some needed warmth to an unfamiliar space. And with all the manual labor they've expended getting the place together, how about giving them a break and putting someone else to work? Lighten their load with the services of a professional handyman. It's exhausting dealing with the pressures of a move, so help your friend settle in swiftly, and let the parties begin!

Dummy Security Camera w/LED

www.x-tremegeek.com

A fake surveillance camera is a lot cheaper than the real thing. This dummy camera has a high-tech design and realistic appearance with a blinking LED, authentic video lens and cable, a fully adjustable mount, and two "Warning" decals. It's made of weatherproof and rustproof anodized aluminum.

Home Sweet Home Gift Basket

www.gothambaskets.com 

Gotham Baskets offers an original housewarming basket that will stand out. The Home Sweet Home basket looks like a white picket fence and is filled with Home Sweet Home cookies, Call It Home snack mix, Housewarming strewing herbs, a chocolate key, Housewarming fortune cookies, coffee, tea, and a canned fruit candle.

"Home Sweet Apartment" Tile

www.ournameismud.com

So what if they don't have a two-car garage. This ceramic tile has a painted cityscape and the saying "Home Sweet Apartment."

Any Bitch Can Fake It Cookbook

www.cookscorner.com 

With a new home, who has time to cook? *Any Bitch Can Fake It* makes it easy for them to throw a feast together for guests who drop by to check out the new place.

Handyman

www.handymanconnection.com prices vary

This national chain will have someone in their area who can come to the rescue. They'll take care of anything from painting and electrical work to basement, bath, and kitchen remodeling.

House Numbers

www.westonletters.com 🎁🎁🎁+

With a variety of styles to choose from, these house numbers will add that finishing touch.

Hawaiian Pineapples

www.dolefruithawaii.com 🎁🎁

Pineapples are a traditional sign of hospitality dating back to Colonial days. This case comes packaged with two Tropical Gold Pineapples right off the Dole plantations in Hawaii.

Black-Eyed Peas

www.bulkfoods.com 🎁/pound

Black-eyed peas are a Southern tradition of hospitality. Buy some in bulk and put them in a decorative gift bag. Attach a handwritten note explaining the history of the tradition.

Chocolate-Covered Pretzels

www.thegreatamericanpretzelcompany.com 🎁

It's an old Russian folk custom to present someone with salt and bread as a sign of hospitality, signifying that you wish for plenty in their pantry. You can add sugar to that to symbolize hopes for a sweet life. Wrap that all up into one delicious treat, and you've got yourself some chocolate-covered pretzels. The Great American Sampler Gift Box comes with pretzel twists and nuggets dressed up with different chocolate coatings, caramel, peanut butter, and nuts.

Tool Kit

www.sears.com

The Craftsman nineteen-piece Homeowner's Tool Kit comes loaded with all the usual suspects they're going to need to get the new place together: a saw, tape measure, hammer, level, wrench, pliers, knife, and screwdrivers. It's all held in a durable soft-sided carrying case.

Personalized Doormat

www.rolandsgifts.com (22" × 36")

Create your own original personalized coir doormat. Choose a name, phrase, or monogram plus your color combination, and drop it off at the feet of the grateful new residents.

Claus Porto Guest Soap Pastilles

www.lafcony.com

Are they candies or soaps? This elegant box of guest soaps has fifteen individual guest soaps shaped like candy pastilles. Soaps are hand stamped and made of 2 percent shea butter. Nine delicious scents to choose from.

Feng Shui for Dummies DVD

www.amazon.com 

This DVD will show them how they can apply feng shui principles to their new home and improve the overall flow and energy throughout the space.

White Sage Smudge Stick

www.wholisticplanetstore.com 🎁

It's an old tradition to burn sage to cleanse a space and get rid of bad spirits and negative energy. Handwrite out instructions for a traditional sage-burning ceremony and attach them to the sage bundle.

Chimes

www.windchime.com 🎁🎁+

Wind chimes bring a soft sound to the new environment. Choose from a selection of chimes in aluminum, glass, ceramic, wood, and brass.

Martha Stewart's *Everyday Food* Subscription

www.marthastewart.com 🎁/ten issues

Once a month, your recipient can look forward to Martha's handy little cookbook—great recipes that address the season and upcoming holidays.

Coffee Table Book

www.taschen.com 🎁🎁

Taschen publishes some of the most beautiful books around, plus they make you feel like you're on a vacation when you're flipping through them. Taschen's *Spa* book takes you on a trip through the world's most fantastic spas. Read and relax.

The Perfect Houseplant

www.whiteflowerfarm.com 🎁🎁

The clivia is one of the easiest plants to care for. With just a little light and some care, this plant will sprout deep green arching leaves and gorgeous orange, lily-shaped blooms in the spring. Plant arrives in a 7" terra-cotta pot with saucer.

In a Jam Gift

www.deborahskitchen.com 🎁🎁

Deborah's Kitchen makes 100 percent fruit spreads in a variety of yummy flavors. A signature wooden gift box features an assortment of her best, including: Forest Berries, Wild Blues, Massachusetts Rubies, Peach Melba, and Mango Sunshine.

Housewarming Cookie "Bouquet"

www.corsoscookies.com 🎁🎁+

Corso's Cookies gift bouquets are made from delicious butter-crème cookies and individually hand-decorated by an icing artist. The Hearty Housewarming collection features cookies in the shape of houses and mailboxes and can be personalized with the new owner's name and address on the cookies.

Monogrammed Pewter Wine Bottle Coaster and Stopper

www.williams-sonoma.com 🎁🎁

This custom monogrammed pewter wine coaster comes with a matching pewter wine stopper. Both are detailed with clusters of grapes.

Stainless Steel Seven-Piece Bar Set

www.williams-sonoma.com 🎁🎁

Toast the new home with this seven-piece Bar Tool Set that comes with a strainer, jigger, bottle opener, bar knife, ice tongs, and stirrer, all held in a convenient stainless caddy.

Egyptian Cotton Monogrammed Guest Towels

www.horchow.com 🎁

These super soft 20" × 32" hand towels come in more than a dozen rich colors and can be monogrammed for your new homeowner.

Homedics Pedicure Pro Foot Spa

www.walmart.com 🎁🎁

After the move, they can pamper their peds with a deluxe Foot Spa and Massager. The quiet spa has a comfort gel footrest and toe-touch control and features "Double the Bubbles" massaging. Accessories include a dry heel reducer, stone pumice, finishing pumice, nail brush, and nail buffer.

Complete Idiot's Guide to Home Repair and Maintenance Illustrated

http://us.penguingroup.com 🎁

Everything they'll need to know for when the sink explodes or the lights go out.

Sleek Serving Set

www.napahometx.com 🎁🎁🎁🎁

The elegant Ercuis Paris Mezzo stainless steel two-piece serving set comes packaged in a stunning blue presentation box.

Crystal Potpourri

www.beautyhabit.com 🎁🎁

The Côté Bastide balls of potpourri are made from resin and sprayed with a blend of vanilla and a signature amber scent.

Hurricane Survival Kit

www.bluecrabbay.com 🎁🎁🎁

Friend moving to a Gulf state? This hurricane survival kit will help them out when the time comes. Large nylon tote comes stuffed with a portable radio/flashlight, an Atlantic Ocean laminated hurricane tracking chart and felt tip pen, a mini first aid kit, and the essential items: Sea Salt Nuts and Sting Ray Bloody Mary Mixer.

Baby Bundt Variety Gift Pack

www.rowenas.com 🎁🎁

An assorted sampler of six-ounce Bundt cakes includes one each of Island Kissed Key Lime, Praline, Zesty Orange Almond, Cranberry Lemon, and Buttered Rum—and comes in a polka-dot gift box.

Homeowner's Record Keeper: The Perfect Place to Keep Track of Home Repairs, Maintenance, Plans, and Dreams (Past & Present)

www.powells.com 🎁

This workbook will help them keep track of home records and maintenance schedules, prioritize repairs and improvements, and plan for future projects.

Field Guide to Tools

www.borders.com 🎁

This handy guide prevents any future embarrassment when confused at the local Home Depot. Over one hundred tools are identified and presented with how-to directions for use.

Chalkboard Napkin Rings

www.sarut.com 🎁

Kill two birds with one stone—these napkin rings double as placeholders—they're mini-chalkboards, so just write the guest's name on the ring.

Scented Drawer Liners

www.elizabethw.com 🎁🎁

Elizabeth W's silk and linen drawer liners will give a sweet scent to anything they tuck away. Scents are lavender, rose, or cedar.

Rose Petal Soaps

www.ebubbles.com 🎁

Fifty individual rose petal single-use soaps come in a clear plastic tube. Each petal dissolves with water and releases a rosy smell.

Mailbox Art Wrap

www.curbdecor.com 🎁

They can have the most original mailbox on the block with a Mail Wrap. Choose from a catalog of designs featuring themes ranging from botanical to seasonal to inspirational. Each wrap is made of sturdy vinyl and attaches to the mailbox with magnets on each side of the cover.

Glass Green Apple

www.artthang.com 🎁🎁🎁

This hand-blown glass apple is a vibrant green and adds color and warmth to any room.

Old-Fashioned First Aid Box

www.themut.com

Just like the commercial ones at school or the office, this latching steel case with a handle will conveniently store away all first aid needs. Fill it with supplies, and they're set. From the Museum of Useful Things.

Compleat Cheese Board and Tools All in One

www.wrapables.com

The 16" × 8.5" bamboo cheese board holds a cheese knife, planer, and spreader in a Lucite case on the underside of the board. Tools are made of stainless steel.

Vanilla Tea Gift

www.harney.com

Along with a new two-cup teapot they'll get a tin of twenty Vanilla Comoro sachets, and three amber sugar stirring sticks.

Decadent Desserts Basket

www.greenmountaincoffee.com

Green Mountain Coffee Roasters offers a gift basket that blends gourmet coffee with some sweets. The Decadent Desserts Basket comes with ten ounces of the Vermont Country Blend, twelve ounces of Hazelnut Cream coffee, a tin of sugar to rim a coffee glass, hazelnut biscotti, and rich Tanzanian Chocolate Sauce from Lake Champlain Chocolates.

Classic Gumball Machine

www.gumballs.com

A gumball machine is a fun toy for every new home. The

Original King Carousel Gumball Machine has a glass globe, all-metal base, lid, and coin mechanism that can be set to Free Spin. It's 15" high and can hold up to four pounds of gumballs (not included).

Gardener's Essential Tool Kit

www.brookstone.com 🎁🎁🎁

They can keep their new garden in good shape with a kit that has everything they could possibly need when digging in the dirt. The tool kit comes with a cultivator, weeder, trowel, planter, dibble, fork, pruning set, six-piece hose connector set, spray nozzles, and a shower/mister.

Monogrammed Bath Rug

www.horchow.com 🎁🎁🎁🎁

Habidecor makes this luxurious cotton bath rug that can be customized with a single initial monogram. Rug measures 20" × 31" and comes in white with a contrasting color for the border and initial. Choose from vanilla, blue, ivory, green, or blush; and style: block or script.

Designer Address Labels

www.thestationerystudio.com 🎁+

They can add some style to the U.S. Postal Service with designer return address labels featuring their new home address. There are lots of styles to choose from: masculine, circular, even personalized family stick figures.

Monogrammed Toilet Paper

www.wishingfish.com 🎁

Feel like royalty when you put out fancy personalized toilet paper for your guests. Or just appreciate it privately. Orders come with two shrink-wrapped rolls, each sporting a single letter.

NYT Recipe Master

www.nytstore.com

This electronic gadget features 1,000 complete recipes from the *New York Times* food editor and master chef Craig Claiborne. It includes a built-in timer, a glossary of cooking terms and tips, measurement equivalencies, and a grocery list feature.

Lotus Nesting Bowls

www.koodekir.com

This elegant set of eight nesting bowls, each shaped like a lotus flower, sit inside each other with delicate precision.

Café Solo

www.scandinaviandetails.com

This sleek Scandinavian design is a new way to brew some java. Add boiling water to coffee grinds inside the glass carafe, mix with the special stirrer, and pour through the funnel-filter spout and stainless steel lid. To keep it warm, it comes with a zip-up neoprene insulator.

Funny Towels

www.kookootowels.com

A good set to get it going—each towel is embroidered with its purpose—"Face," "Body," "Feet," and "Hands."

Disposable Place Mats

www.cocoacrayon.com

Bob's Your Uncle makes disposable 11" × 17" place mats

adorned with bright dots and humorous recipes written by a real kid. Each package contains forty-eight mats with six different designs.

Money Pots

www.terramundiusa.com 🎁🎁

It's an ancient Italian tradition to add change to a money pot until it is full, then to break it open and spend the savings on something special. These handmade pots are about 17" tall, brightly decorated, and will hold approximately $500 in change when full.

Shiny Silver Mr. Ice Bucket

www.target.com 🎁🎁

Silver metal ice bucket with a silver plastic lid has a three-quart capacity.

Mini Bloomin' Garden Stakes

www.notneutral.com 🎁🎁

Liven up the garden with these candy-colored Bloomin' Garden Stakes featuring blossoms and animals. Boxed set comes with six stakes.

Cookie-of-the-Month Club

www.byrdcookiecompany.com 🎁🎁🎁🎁/twelve months

Gourmet cookies from the Byrd Cookie Company arrive every month in a designer package. Some flavors they can look forward to include chocolate mint cookies, key lime coolers, and butter thins.

Cake Candles

www.gabbygoodies.com 🎁

Gabby Goodies makes candles that look and smell like they're fresh out of the oven. Choose from Cinnamon Bun, Snickerdoodle, or Evening Mocha.

Provence Santé Hand Soaps

www.baudelairesoaps.com 🎁

Packaged in a beautiful box with an artful photograph, this set of four hand soaps makes a gorgeous housewarming gift. Choose from eight luxurious scents.

Twenty-two-Piece Stainless Steel Grill Set

www.sharperimage.com 🎁🎁🎁

All packaged in a hard aluminum case, this master chef grill set includes a monster spatula with serrated cutting edges and a built-in bottle opener, a pair of extra-long tongs, a big grill fork, a carving knife, a basting brush, four skewers, a bristly brush for scraping the grill clean, four pairs of corncob holders, and four stainless steel steak knives.

THE RESTLESS RETIREE

Retirement is bittersweet. On one hand, it's nice to reach the finish line and relax in Permanent Vacationville . . . but on the other hand, what on earth are they supposed to do with all this free time? There's no more heading off to work each morning, finding pleasure in a well-earned position of authority, or hustling to places they "need to be." No—their routine is caput, and the only constants in this new life are trips to the fridge and afternoon talk shows. The Restless Retiree rejects this trap and instead vows to stay active and keep sharp. Now is the time for them to find a new hobby or get reacquainted with an old one. You can get them started with the necessary equipment or professional guidance. If their home is their castle, then indulge them in comfort with homebound spa luxuries and lush trappings. If money is no object, you can always set their imaginations sailing on an extravagant vacation of a lifetime. Or present them with a sentimental keepsake that honors their life and many achievements. The Restless Retiree just wants to keep living life with a purpose. But before you sign them up for hours of free babysitting, don't forget this is *their* retirement, and there's only so much even *they* can take of the grandkids.

Comfy Throw

www.plushnecessities.com 🎁🎁🎁

The Plush Dream Throw is decadently cozy and impossible to take off. Made of a dual-sided superfine microfiber fabric, the throw is trimmed with a matching satin. Size is 54" × 72" and the color choices are merlot or latte.

Membership to a Books on Tape/CD Club

www.simplyaudiobooks.com 🎁+/month

Sign the retiree up for a year's worth of books on tape. Simply Audiobooks has a rental club where you can choose from over 7,500 book titles. They can receive up to four selections at a time, shipping is free both ways, there are no late fees or due dates, and once they're done, they just pop it back in the mail to return.

Astronomy Lesson Telescope

www.hammacher.com 🎁🎁🎁🎁

This easy-to-use telescope is preprogrammed with 20,000 celestial objects and features an automatic track-and-find ability. Once an object is located, the telescope's speaker provides facts about what you are seeing in a human voice.

Ragg Wool Men's Slipper Socks

www.orvis.com 🎁🎁

These cozy winter slippers pull on like socks but have a sturdy leather sidewall and suede bottoms.

Golf Ball Monogrammer

www.orvis.com 🎁

This titanium-finish press comes with two sets of interchangeable letters to brand golf balls with a monogram up to three initials.

Cover of *Retired Living* Magazine

www.personalcreations.com 🎁🎁

It looks real, right? Have a personal photograph turned into what looks to be an actual cover of *Retired Living* magazine. The retiree's name and date of retirement can be included on the cover; as are funny headlines like "The Trouble with Retirement: You Never Get a Day Off!" Print arrives framed in a black 11" × 14" wooden frame.

Ultimate Bingo Party Game

www.homecasinogames.com 🎁🎁

It's time to get the buddies over for some B-I-N-G-O! This deluxe set comes with a large vinyl-coated metal bingo ball cage, seventy-five numbered bingo balls, eighteen cardboard stock bingo cards, a bingo masterboard, and three hundred plastic chips.

Sofa Arm Organizer

www.taylorgifts.com 🎁

This convenient sofa arm storage container keeps essentials organized and within reach. Six pockets are designed to hold everything from remote controls to glasses to magazines . . . there's even a tray top for food and drinks.

Exotic Adventure

www.gapadventures.com 🎁🎁🎁🎁🎁

G.A.P. Adventures offers hundreds of exciting adventure vacations to choose from on seven continents. Their mission is to create adventures in locales that respect the people and land where they travel and to provide authentic experiences to travelers wanting to immerse themselves in another culture. This means trips can take you on everything from a 2,200-mile cruise down the Amazon to a fifteen-day Peruvian trek that takes you deep into the Inca empire and hiking Machu Picchu to a weeklong sailing adventure along the southern coast of Turkey in the Aegean Sea.

Photo Phone

www.goldviolin.com 🎁🎁

Slip up to nine photos of the people they call most often into this phone's quick-dial buttons, and they can call with one push. Phone also features extra-large high-contrast buttons, an illuminated emergency button, hearing aid compatible handset, bright Amplify On, ring flasher, and Hold indicator lights on the base of the phone.

Sudoku Brainteaser Book

http://shop.npr.org 🎁

Sudoku is a wordless crossword puzzle that has obsessed fans around the world. In *The Giant Book of Sudoku*, *New York Times* crossword puzzle editor Will Shortz has assembled three hundred Sudoku games with a varying range of difficulty.

AARP Membership

www.aarp.org 🎁🎁/three-year membership

Give the gift of membership to the AARP, and you'll be providing them with countless discounts on travel, shopping, insurance, and leisure activities, as well as tips for how their lives can be lived to the fullest now that they're retired.

Talking Alarm Clock

www.goldviolin.com 🎁

In case they're feeling a little blurry in the morning, this digital alarm clock lights up and announces the time out loud.

Velvet Foot Cozys

www.goldviolin.com 🎁🎁

These comfy booties can be warmed up in the microwave to keep your toes warm or battle arthritis pain. They include removable aromatherapy packs that are filled with cinnamon to calm, clove for comfort, and eucalyptus to energize. They come in sage green and are available in both men's and women's sizes.

Too Young To Retire

http://us.penguingroup.com 🎁

Too Young to Retire is a perfect book to help a retiree pinpoint the interests they want to focus on in their new lives of leisure. This guide includes exercises and workbook pages as well as a comprehensive list of publications, home exchange organizations, and websites to help make meaningful choices.

Two-Hole Putting Green

www.brookstone.com 🎁🎁🎁🎁🎁

They can practice their shots on this 8' × 10' all-weather putting green. Two regulation cups and club-quality turf will help hone their skills for the course.

Castles and Kilts Golf Cruise

www.crystalcruises.com 🎁🎁🎁🎁🎁

Crystal Cruises offers a deluxe golf-themed cruise called Castles and Kilts that drops passengers off at up to six world-renowned golf courses across Scotland, Ireland, and England. They get the comfort of a luxury cruise and convenience of preplanned golf excursions.

Memory Lane Print

www.yourmemorylane.com 🎁🎁🎁🎁 (unframed)

A Memory Lane print is a personalized, one-of-a-kind work of art to celebrate a special person. It starts with a base of a colorful hand-drawn street with eight buildings and features up to forty-eight personal memories added in along the road. For retirement, you can provide images and words related to events, companies, and people the retiree encountered over the course of a career. The print measures 11½" × 25¾". Smaller prints with fewer buildings are available as well.

Story of a Lifetime

www.redenvelope.com 🎁🎁🎁

This do-it-yourself memoir is bound in a sturdy leather cover and is full of nearly four hundred pages of family information. Over five hundred questions are asked, and you write in the answers to everything from your family tree lineage dating back generations and traditional family recipes to deeper ponderings like "What do you feel has been your purpose in life?" and "Is there any particular incident in your life that changed everything?" This is a great way to pass every bit of information about the family on to future generations.

Oprah's Book-of-the-Month Club

www.bestsellers-monthly-book-connection.com 🎁+

Sign someone up to receive recommendations from Oprah's book club. Each month, they'll receive a new book from the recent selections available.

Almost Golf Practice Stick

www.discountgolfworld.com 🎁🎁

Takes the bending out of retrieving your golf balls. This handy stick picks them up and stores them without a person ever having to lean over.

Golf Bag Cart

www.discountgolfworld.com 🎁🎁🎁🎁

This cart makes it easy to move from one hole to the next without having to carry a heavy golf bag. The Bag Boy EZ Fold LX rides on small bicycle-like tires, has an adjustable handle and bag brackets, a brake and parking system, plus comes with separate holders for a cup, umbrella, and scorecard.

The Autobiography Box

www.vickerey.com 🎁

Now that they have time, they can write their own memoirs. The Autobiography Box is a step-by-step kit including a book and cards filled with quotes, questions, directions, and exercises designed to let you examine your life.

Slot Machine

www.pokerchest.com 🎁🎁🎁🎁

The Dream Max 7 Skill Stop Slot Machine lets you control when the wheels stop. Machine features spinning wheels, flashing lights, and exciting sounds, just like in Vegas. Freight is an extra charge.

Disposable Luggage Tags

www.mosmyownspace.com 🎁

With all their new time to travel, they can keep life exciting and full of attitude with smart-ass luggage tags. Made from leather, these tags have quips like “I’m pretty sure this isn’t your bag,” “Nothing worth stealing in here,” “This is my bag,” and “This is not your suitcase.” Flip it over and there’s room for your personal info. Comes as a set of five tags.

"Pills" Clock

www.wrapables.com 🎁🎁

Remind them to take their medicine with a clock featuring colorful pills instead of numbers.

Retirement Golf Balls

www.enjoylifeinc.com 🎁

These golf balls celebrate retirement with the saying “Full Swing Retirement.” Comes as a pack of three balls.

"Do Not Forget!" Door Hanger

www.mxyplyzyk.com 🎁

Write a note and hang it on a doorknob. Nothing will ever be left behind again.

Monogrammed Playing Cards

www.personalizationmall.com 🎁/single deck

When they host a card game, they can pull out What a Deal! custom monogrammed playing cards. Choose from five different card colors and thirteen different monogram styles or create a custom message in one of three lettering styles. Standard-sized casino-quality cards come packaged in a handsome gift box.

Mah-Jongg Set

www.mahjonggmaven.com 🎁🎁🎁

Mah-jongg is an ancient Chinese game played with tiles. American Mah Jongg Sets come in a variety of cases with trays for tiles. Tiles are nonfading, engraved, and painted. Some sets includes extra tiles, racks, dice, bettor, chips, and an instruction book.

Pedometer and Walking Book

www2.oregonscientific.com 🎁

Now they have plenty of opportunity to get in shape. The lightweight Oregon Scientific Digital Pedometer will measure the number of steps taken, distance walked, calories burned, and time elapsed. It has a high-glow backlight for easy reading and comes with the book *Walk Yourself Thin* to help track the workouts.

Tea-of-the-Month Club

www.adagio.com 🎁🎁+

Pick a Tea Plan from Fruit, Herbal, DeCaf, Black, or Oolong/Green gourmet teas, and they'll receive a four-ounce tin each month with a new tea to taste. They'll also receive Adagio's trademark IngenuiTEA Teapot. Just add loose tea to hot water in the pot; then when it's steeped long enough, place over mug, release valve, and the tea pours down right into the mug.

Eyewitness to History: Walter Cronkite Remembers Video Set

www.nytstore.com 🎁🎁

Walter Cronkite shares his eyewitness experiences to the twentieth century in this seven-video set. The tapes feature rare historic film and newsreel clips and photos and covers the Great Depression, organized crime, World War I and II, the Cold War, civil rights, women's rights, the space race, Kennedy's assassination, and much more.

Puzzlemaster Collection

http://shop.npr.org 🎁🎁

From the National Public Radio store, this gift pack for puzzlers includes Will Shortz's *Puzzlemaster* books, volumes 1 and 2, plus a sixteen-ounce ceramic mug and refillable mechanical pencil.

Stainless Steel Bird Feeder

www.retromodern.com 🎁🎁🎁🎁

Retirement is for the birds. This ultramodern bird feeder by Mono Studio is made of stainless steel and glass and has a striking architectural design.

Signature Themed Pens

www.joshbach.com 🎁🎁

Forget about ordinary pens; these rollerballs have a black lacquer finish and handcrafted nickel-silver clips that discreetly and stylishly celebrate sports, hobbies, and professions. You'll find everything from a baseball bat to a toothbrush to a shotgun. Each pen comes packaged in an individual wooden case.

ABOUT THE AUTHOR

Sarah Weidman has been a producer and development executive in reality television at companies that include MTV, Sony Pictures Television, and the Style Network. She has been featured as the "Go-to Gift Guru" for KCBS News in Los Angeles and spends her free time on the hunt for the latest-and-greatest products and services.